the **thrill** of the **chaste**

the thrill of the chaste

finding fulfillment while keeping your clothes on

Dawn Eden

W PUBLISHING GROUP
A Division of Thomas Nelson Publishers
Since 1798

www.wpublishinggroup.com

Published by W Publishing Group, a division of Thomas Nelson, Inc., P.O. Box 141000, Nashville, Tennessee 37214.

Scripture quotations noted NIV are from The Holy Bible, New International Version (NIV). Copyright © 1973, 1978, 1984, International Bible Society. Used by permission of Zondervan Bible Publishers.

Scripture quotations noted NKJV are from The New King James Version (NKJV®), copyright 1979, 1980, 1982, Thomas Nelson, Inc., Publishers.

Scripture quotations noted KJV are from the King James Version of the Bible.

Library of Congress Cataloging-in-Publication Data

Eden, Dawn, 1968–
    The thrill of the chaste / Dawn Eden.
      p. cm.
    ISBN-10: 0-8499-1311-X
    ISBN-13: 978-0-8499-1311-2
    1. Single women—Religious life. 2. Single women—Conduct of life.
3. Single women—Sexual behavior. 4. Christian women—Conduct of life.
5. Chastity. 6. Sexual abstinence—Religious aspects—Christianity. I. Title.
BV4596.S5E34 2006
241'.66—dc22

                                       2006012959

Printed in the United States of America

06 07 08 09 RRD 5 4 3 2 1

To Mary and Maximilian,
with gratitude for your inspiring examples
and prayers.

contents

introduction

Chastity, like me, has long suffered from a bad reputation—only in chastity's case, it's undeserved.

For me, it began as an experiment. I'd hit my mid-thirties. I knew that I wanted to be married. I also knew that sex à la New York City—bowing to urges and temptations, rushing into sex in the hope that love would develop, or using sex in the hope of landing a commitment—wasn't cutting it. I saw myself sliding into middle age on a slimy slope of cynicism, resentment, and loneliness.

The immediate advantage of chastity was a sense of control. True, my cynical side—which was suppressed but not down for the count—would have had me believe that what seemed like self-control was really just that I couldn't get a date. But in reality, I knew that I often passed up sexual opportunities that I would have grabbed in the days when my central desire was to ease my loneliness.

As time passed, however, another, clearer advantage came into view. It was the realization that all the sex I had ever had—in and out of relationships—never brought me any closer to marriage or even being able to sustain a committed relationship.

How was I to know any better? I had dutifully followed the *Cosmo* rule, which is also the *Sex and the City* rule and really the Universal Single-Person Rule in our secular age: "Sex should push the relationship." This rule can also be expressed as, "We'll talk about it in bed."

But it's worse than that. By viewing sex as a means to an end rather than the fruit of a loving relationship, I rendered myself incapable of *having* a loving relationship.

Love—the true love that comes from God—requires pure motives.

There's no question that in God's eyes, sex is a good thing—and, as I'll explain in Chapter 7, that's putting it mildly. What is not good is having it for the wrong reasons—such as considering another person's mind, spirit, or body as something to possess or enjoy, rather than the whole person as some*one* to actively love.

This objectification can be unconscious. I know I have never intentionally set out to use anyone. But we are judged by our fruit. The fruit of casual sex is the persistent habit of objectifying sexual partners, to the point of being unable to perceive people except in terms of how they relate to one's own wants and desires.

When I started on this chastity kick three years ago—or even today, at bedtime when I try to stop myself from fantasizing about someone I'd like to objectify—I would wonder, in the words of Jesus's disciples, "Who then can be saved?" (Mark 10:26 NKJV).

Jesus's answer to that question remains as mysterious and tantalizing today as it was nearly two thousand years ago: "With men it is impossible, but not with God; for with God all things are possible" (10:27 NKJV).

When we ask God for help, He gives us more grace, knowledge, wisdom, and spiritual understanding. Much of the time, it's only enough light to show us the next step. But at times of trial and temptation, that may be all that's needed to get through the darkness safely.

I don't have a potential boyfriend at the moment, but even so, I believe that right now I am closer than ever before to being not only married but *happily* married.

I'm sure that sounds outrageously optimistic, if not downright irrational, to someone who believes the only way to get married is to be sexually available. Yet, I can write with authority, because I've experienced nonmarital sex and I've experienced chastity, and I know what lies at the core of each.

Both experiences are centered on a kind of faith. One of them, sex before marriage, relies on faith that a man who has not shown faith in you—that is, not enough faith to commit himself to you for life—will come around through the persuasive force of your physical affection. It forces you to follow a set of Darwinian social rules—dressing and acting a certain way to outperform other women competing for mates. A man who's attracted to you will eventually learn who you really are—but by then, if all goes according to the rules, your hooks will be in too deep for him to escape.

The other experience, chastity, relies on faith that God, as you pursue a closer walk with Him, will lead you to a loving husband. Chastity opens up your world, enabling you to achieve your creative and spiritual potential without the pressure of having to play the dating game. Your husband will love you for yourself—your heart, mind, body, and soul.

When faced with a choice between two attitudes—both of which require looking beyond present reality—I choose the one that has a solid foundation. Chastity's foundation is faith in God—the kind of faith that Scripture says "is the substance of things hoped for, the evidence of things not seen" (Hebrews 11:1 NKJV). Your faith acts as a gateway to God's grace, enabling Him to give you strength and resilience greater than you could imagine having on your own.

Perhaps you, like me, don't have a special man in your life right now. Even so, when you put on chastity, you'll discover a life more hope-filled, more vibrant, more *real* than anything you might have experienced when having sex outside of marriage. *That* is the thrill of the chaste.

not the same old song

Late one night, walking home from my newspaper job, I passed by a Johnny Rockets—the chain of Fifties-style burger joints—just as it was closing. As the bored waiters in their starched white uniforms and matching caps wiped the chrome tabletops, one last jukebox tune crackled from the outdoor speakers onto the deserted streets: the Shirelles' "Will You Love Me Tomorrow."

The song brought up bittersweet memories—more bitter than sweet. Like many songs from that more innocent era, "Will You Love Me Tomorrow" expresses feelings that most people would be too ashamed to verbalize. There's something painful about the way its vulnerable heroine leaves herself wide open. She's not looking for affirmation so much as absolution. All her man has to do is say he loves her—then a night of sin is transformed into a thing of beauty.

Do you believe that you have the right to own an Uzi? If you're a staunch defender of the Second Amendment, maybe you do—

1

aftert all, the right to bear arms is in the United States Constitution. But having the right to own one doesn't mean you necessarily should—and you might not like to live in a place where people tote them around.

Likewise, the pursuit of happiness is in the Constitution—and it's safe to say that many single women in the New York City area where I live believe that part of that right is an active sex life. Magazines like *Cosmopolitan*, many TV shows from *Oprah* on down, as well as films, books, and pop songs urge single women to take the sexual pleasure that's due them. While love is celebrated, women are told that a satisfying sexual "hookup" does not require love— only respect. If "R-E-S-P-E-C-T" was good enough for Sixties soul diva Aretha Franklin, it's supposed to be good enough for us too.

The fruits of this accepted single-woman lifestyle resemble those of a drug habit more than a dating paradigm. In a vicious cycle, single women feel lonely because they are not loved, so they have casual sex with men who do not love them.

That was my life.

At age twenty, when I was still a virgin, I lost my beloved boyfriend to a sexually experienced friend who seduced him. He had been a long-distance beau for two years, and I'd dreamed of having him live nearby. When he finally moved to New York City, just across Central Park from my apartment, we celebrated together. Then, a mere month later, he sprang the news that he was breaking up with me. At the time, he denied there was another woman, but eventually he admitted to me that he had lied, hoping to let me down easy. As it turned out, my friend had come on to him—and he'd left me for her.

The crushing blow convinced me that I had to gain experience if I wanted to hold a man. I wound up losing my virginity to a man I found attractive but didn't love—just to get my card punched.

Once I became experienced, instead of being supremely self-confident, I only became more insecure. I learned that if I played my cards right, I could get almost any man I wanted into bed—but when it came to landing a boyfriend, the deck was always stacked against me.

No matter how hard I tried, I couldn't transform a sexual encounter—or a string of encounters—into a real relationship. The most I could hope for, it seemed, was a man who would treat me with "respect," but who really wouldn't have any concern for me once we split the tab for breakfast.

That's not to say I didn't meet any nice guys while I was casually dating. I did, but either they seemed boring—as nice guys so often are when you're used to players—or I KO'd the budding relationship by trying to rush things.

Don't get me wrong; I wasn't insatiable. I was insecure.

When you're insecure, you fear losing control. In my case, the main way I thought I could control a relationship was by either introducing a sexual component or allowing my boyfriend to do so. Either way, I would end up alone and unhappy—but I didn't know how else to handle a relationship. I felt trapped in a lifestyle that gave me none of the things that the media and popular wisdom promised it would.

Some friends and family, trying to be helpful, would counsel me to simply stop looking. I did manage to stop looking, sometimes for months at a time—but then, when I would meet a potential boyfriend, I'd once again bring the relationship down to the lowest common denominator.

I hated the seeming inevitability of it all—how all my attempts at relationships would crash and burn—yet, in some strange way, it seemed safe. By speeding things up sexually, I was saving myself from being rejected—or worse, ignored—if I moved too slowly. And after all, if I was eventually going to be rejected anyway, I thought I should at least get something out of it—if only a night of sex.

It all sounds terribly cynical, thinking back on it now, and it was. I was lonely and depressed, and I had painted myself into a corner.

∽◦∾

In October 1999, at the age of thirty-one, my life changed radically when, after being an agnostic Jew for my entire adult life, I had what Christians would call a born-again experience. Having read the Gospels, I had long believed that Jesus was a good man. What changed me was realizing for the first time that He was more than a man—He was truly God's Son.

With my newfound Christian faith came a sudden awareness that I badly needed to "get with the program"—especially where my sex life was concerned. But even being aware of what had to be done, I had a long way to go between realizing what was wrong with my behavior and actually changing it.

Thankfully, over time, I found that whenever I was tempted to return to the vicious cycle (meet intriguing guy/have sex/dump or be dumped/repeat), a new thought would emerge to give me pause—an antidote to the pleasure principle. I call it the tomorrow principle.

∽◦∾

All my adult life, I've struggled with my weight. When I'm walking home at the end of the day, there's nothing I want more than a bag of Cheez Doodles or malted-milk balls. If I'm trying to slim down—which is most of the time—it's hard, really hard, to think of why I can't have what I'm craving.

The little devil on my left shoulder is saying, "Get the Cheez

Doodles. You'll be satisfied, and you won't gain weight. Even if you do gain, it'll be less than a pound—you can lose it the next day."

And you know what? He's right. If I look at it in a vacuum, one indiscretion is not going to do any damage that can't be undone.

Then the little angel on my right shoulder speaks up. "Uh-uh. If you buy those Cheez Doodles, you know what's going to happen."

"I'll get orange fingerprints on the pages of the novel I'm reading tonight?" I reply.

The angel lets that one go by. "You'll buy them again tomorrow night," he nags. "And the next night.

"Remember what happened during the fall of your freshman year of high school," the angel goes on, "when the student clubs held after-school bake sales every day? Remember how you discovered that if you waited around long enough, all the goodies would be discounted 'til you could get five Toll House cookies for a quarter?"

"Please—" I groan. I know where this is going. The devil on my left shoulder is pulling my hair in the direction of the snack-foods aisle.

"And remember," the angel continues, smelling victory, "how your jeans kept getting tighter and tighter? And you had to—"

"I *know*," I say, exasperatedly.

"You had to lie down to zip them up," he says triumphantly. "Finally, one by one, you busted the fly on *every pair of jeans you owned*."

By that point, the devil has usually fled, and I am left looking for a nice, dry, fat-free, high-fiber bran muffin. But I am not happy. Quite the contrary—I feel deprived.

That's how I used to feel before I understood the meaning of chastity—when I was following friends' and relatives' advice to "stop looking." I knew some of the negative reasons for forgoing dates with men who were out for casual sex—such encounters would make me feel used and leave me lonelier than before—but I lacked positive reasons.

To lose weight without feeling deprived takes more than just listening to the warnings of the angel on my shoulder. It takes a positive vision. I have to imagine how I'll look and feel far into the future—not just tomorrow, but tomorrow and tomorrow and tomorrow. I have to widen my perspective and see the cumulative effect of temptation: every time I give in, it wears down my resistance, but every time I resist, I grow stronger.

The tomorrow principle requires that vision to be able to see how chastity will help me become the strong, sensitive, confident woman I so long to be. I hate acting out of desperation, feeling as if I have to give of myself physically because it's the only way to reach a man emotionally. And I hate feeling so lonely that I have to take caresses and kisses from a man who essentially views me as a piece of meat—a rare and attractive piece of meat, deserving of the highest respect, but meat nonetheless. I long with all my heart to be able to look beyond my immediate desires, conducting myself with the grace and wisdom that will ultimately bring me fulfillment not just for a night, but for a lifetime.

❧

I first discovered the value of the tomorrow principle late one night in the spring of 2002, as I was preparing to leave a party in a Brooklyn apartment. The host, Steve—a quirky musician with a bashful, puppy-dog face like *Friends* star David Schwimmer or *Graduate*-era Dustin Hoffman—was an acquaintance I'd known for years, though never very well. We'd long had a mild flirtation going, but nothing had come of it because we didn't really have much in common other than physical attraction. So I was caught off guard when he asked me if I'd like to stay the night.

My first thought was an image of the long, scary, late-night subway ride home, contrasted with the appeal of sharing Steve's bed. I thought about how he would kiss me, and how we'd joke and giggle as we experienced the novelty of being naked together. In my mind's eye, I could see his shoulders silhouetted against the gray morning light filtering in through the curtains during the one hour of the day when his bustling neighborhood fell quiet.

It was things like that—the easy camaraderie, the breaking down of boundaries, the fleeting romantic moments—that I really looked forward to in casual-sex encounters. The sex itself, I knew, could be hit-or-miss.

As my mind ran through the possibilities, I remembered that my spiritual situation had changed since the last time I'd received such an offer. I was a baby Christian now, still wet behind the ears, and I knew I wanted my life to reflect my faith. But what made me tell Steve no wasn't the force of conviction. It was another vision that flashed through my brain, sharper than the first—as though it had actually happened.

In that vision, I saw myself and Steve the next morning, at a diner. It wasn't a Johnny Rockets, but a bona fide old-fashioned greasy spoon in his neighborhood. I was wearing the same jeans and purple velvet blouse I had worn to the party. My hair was still a little wet from showering, and it was poking out in all the wrong directions—it doesn't hold up well when I don't use conditioner.

We were having breakfast and trying to talk about something light, as if we'd just happened to run into each other at 10:00 a.m.

on a Sunday. In front of me was the same morning meal I always order at a New York diner: poached eggs on dry rye toast, no potatoes, and coffee with skim milk.

The image was pathetic.

Just the idea of one more uncomfortable morning-after breakfast, my loveless partner oozing with "respect"—that is, what qualifies as respect in the casual-dating world ("I'll still respect you")—was more than I could bear.

But the vision also had a more insidious quality, which I can describe only as grotesque. Here I was, so choosy that I insisted on four different specifications on my diner breakfast. Yet, I couldn't hold out for the one man with whom I could share *every* breakfast for the rest of my life?

The Shirelles' "Will You Love Me Tomorrow" suggests that a night of sex is redeemed if the couple declares after the fact that they love each other. The concept is also a popular theme in romance novels, TV shows, and movies—think *Pretty Woman*. People buy into such a fantasy because they want to believe that objectifying someone else is excusable.

Yet, in my vision of breakfast with Steve, even if he suddenly professed his undying love as I bit into my egg on toast, it wouldn't change the decision I'd made the night before—to sleep with him not because I loved him, but just because I could. And I then realized that if I wound up loving him back, it wouldn't change the fact that twelve hours earlier I'd intended to use him and be used.

If we ever got married, that would be our story—we were acquainted without being good friends, "hooked up" one night after having a few drinks, and fell in love.

Somehow, I don't think that's a recipe for a lasting marriage. If having sex with me were enough to make my husband fall in love, he might go on to have sex with another woman and fall in love with her too.

Likewise, if I were that easily swayed by a roll in the hay, I'd be liable to run off with the proverbial pizza deliveryman. But that's silly—I'm not like that, and I knew I'd be no more likely to fall in love with Steve after sex than I was at that moment. I would, however, feel more attached to him, even if it wasn't love. Sex does that to me whether I want it to or not; it's part of how I'm wired as a woman. That sense of attachment would make the separation after breakfast that much harder.

Once that image entered my mind, the choice was clear.

I thanked Steve for a lovely party and left. Somewhere during the journey from the midnight Brooklyn streets to my New Jersey apartment, I think I cried. Turning down intimacy—even the wrong kind—can hit hard when you're coming home to an empty place.

But I don't regret it. And I've lived by the tomorrow principle ever since.

If you have to ask someone if he'll still love you tomorrow, then he doesn't love you tonight.

two

sex and the witty:
getting a rise out of chastity

The first period of time in my adult life that I was chaste on purpose—and by chaste, I mean not engaging in much more than some kissing here and there (with both "here" and "there" located on my lips)—lasted just over two years, from 2000 through 2001. The reasons for it were the same as they are now—a desire to remain pure for my husband, and an aversion to the objectification and compartmentalization that casual sex requires.

When I look back on those two years now, I can remember only two stages:

1. the "I'm fine, really; I've got so much going on in my life, and God is good—He's taken away my longing, which is something I couldn't do for myself" stage

2. the "climbing the walls" stage

As I recall, the "climbing the walls" stage took up the beginning and the end of the two years, while the "I'm fine" stage took up a few precious months in the middle.

Now that I'm going the chastity route again, I find that my memory oversimplified things. Within those two stages are a myriad of subdivisions.

The subdivision that I am in right now is the "This is a joke" stage—but before you jump to conclusions, allow me to explain.

I've realized that there is a difference between the loneliness and frustration I feel now and the kind I felt from my teens through my early thirties, before I had faith. Back then, I believed that life was a joke, and the joke was on me.

Now, I realize that life as a chaste single woman is indeed a joke—and I'm in on it.

So much of Christianity is about paradoxes, like Jesus's saying, "Whosoever will lose his life for my sake shall find it" (Matthew 16:25 KJV), or God's telling Paul, "My strength is made perfect in weakness" (2 Corinthians 12:9 NKJV). There's a cosmic absurdity to being an immaterial soul in a material body, a Spirit-driven creature in a flesh-driven world.

Likewise, it seems absurd to me that I should be who I am—in my mid-thirties and still single. That I show up at parties without a date. And that my singlehood should ultimately be by choice—because I have a definite idea of the kind of man I seek, and I haven't met him yet.

It's absurd, because it's not how the world works. If you're a woman, you're supposed to be married by the time you're thirty. And if you're not married, you're supposed to, in the words of a personal-ad Web site's slogan, "make your married friends jealous"—compensating for your isolation via cynical casual-sex encounters, like the lost souls of *Sex and the City*.

In the eyes of *Sex and the City* heroine Carrie Bradshaw and friends, as well as much of the culture that made author Candace Bushnell's book and TV show famous, a single woman who chooses chastity over, say, a furtive fumble with a handsome hedonist is either a masochist, a prude, or simply not in her right mind.

Sometimes I wonder myself why I do it. It's hard to pass up opportunities for no-strings sex. When I have a boyfriend, as I did for six months last year, it's even harder to keep in mind why it's important to me to remain chaste until marriage.

The incongruity of the situation is even more striking when I think about what my life would have been like had I been born during my mother's time. Sure, there were "bad girls" in the Fifties, but saving sex for marriage was nonetheless considered a worthy and attainable goal.

Think about it! America's sweetheart was Doris Day—the sexy blonde singer and actress who, in the words of film critic David Thomson, "played career women that acted like coy ingénues in what were supposed to be sophisticated comedies."[1]

During the time of Day's most popular films—the Fifties through the mid-Sixties—her onscreen purity was so legendary that Hollywood wit Oscar Levant famously quipped, "I knew Doris Day before she was a virgin."[2] Yet, audiences didn't want her any other way. Women adored how Day appeared bold, independent, willing to take risks, and totally in control of herself. Men simply adored her.

It was the last time chastity was cool.

Here in the twenty-first century, trying to be like Doris Day—

sexy yet modest, confident yet humble, lighthearted yet deep—is simply unhip. However, it's so unhip that it's considered downright *subversive*.

∽∾

While pundits were quick to poke fun at Day's purported purity, one thing they never called her was "celibate."

Back in the Fifties, only Catholic priests and other religious were "celibate." Those who reserved sex for eventual marriage were "virgins" or simply "chaste."

"Celibate" came to replace "chaste" during the sexual revolution of the Sixties and Seventies—just as people lost sight of what chastity was.

After all, celibacy is easy to understand—and easier still to lampoon. Celibates don't have sex. Period.

In recent years, celibacy came to be used as a shield by pop stars unwilling to "come out." When I was in college, I asked my friend Luba, who had a crush on the Smiths' lead singer, Morrissey, how she felt about her idol's being a gay icon.

"He's not *gay*," she said defensively. "He's said that he's *celibate*."

Compared to celibacy, the concept of chastity contains nuances that are utterly confusing to the modern mind. Its very nature goes against popularly held beliefs about not only sex but the human will in general.

What exactly is chastity, then, if not merely abstaining from sex?

The best short definition I've seen is by Dr. Mark Lowery, associate professor of theology at the University of Dallas. He says it is "that virtue by which we are in control of our sexual appetite rather than it being in control of us."[3]

In a larger sense, chastity is seeing your sexual nature as part of a three-way relationship—and no, that isn't what it sounds like. The

14

relationship is between you, your husband—or, if you're not married, your future husband—and God. That means if you have sex without one corner of that triangle in place—with a man who isn't your husband, or with your husband but without faith in God—the act becomes disconnected from its purpose.

This disconnectedness leads to what writer John Zmirak has called a sort of spiritual bulimia.[4] In attempting to escape loneliness, we accept a sexual act devoid of spiritual nourishment. Such nourishment can come only from the union of two permanently committed souls.

I can't speak for men, but I know from experience that, for a woman, the disconnected feeling that premarital sex brings can be emotionally disastrous. When you're not having sex within the essential union of yourself, your husband, and God, you're really having sex only with yourself. You're projecting your own hopes and dreams onto your sex partner—and setting yourself up for heartbreak.

I know this because the best sex I ever had was with a man who didn't love me—and who lost interest in me immediately afterward.

I had been dating "Jasper" intermittently for several months, always hoping he would get serious. He seemed to think of me only as a good-time pal, a pretty face he could take to dinner and impress with stories of his high-powered media job.

Deep down, I knew Jasper was too distant and too much of a boaster to open his heart to me. But, perhaps partly because my father had been absent during my childhood, I'd always had a thing for distant men. I felt if I could win Jasper over, it would somehow give me a sense of personal validation.

When his birthday came around, I took it as an opportunity to ask Jasper if I could take *him* to dinner. We went to a steak house in his neighborhood, and somehow we decided together that afterward I would spend the night at his place. (I can't recall exactly what was said, but I'm sure I was hinting broadly that I wouldn't object to an overnight invitation.) Finally, I thought, my chance had come.

He wasn't a great lover. Somehow, I knew he wouldn't be—whenever we went out, he never seemed to care if I was having a good time. But when we had sex, something happened to me. I felt physically . . . *different*. It wasn't like we were just two separate bodies. It was as though we completed each other. The feeling brought on a sense of euphoria, affecting me in a way that was, I thought, intensely spiritual.

The whole experience was mystifying to me, because deep down I was aware that even if Jasper decided he wanted a committed relationship, he wasn't capable of being the kind of boyfriend I needed. He was not the type to give of himself. Knowing that there was no real spiritual connection between us, and yet feeling a connection with him through having sex, was deeply confusing.

Jasper's subsequent behavior bore out my fears. From the moment I left his apartment, he carried on as though our night together had never happened.

So why, then, did I feel what I felt when Jasper and I had sex? Why do I still miss that feeling, even though I don't really miss him?

Because I wasn't really having sex with him; I was having sex with my fantasy of him. The sheer shock of getting to be physically intimate with a man who had acted so distant made me imagine an emotional intimacy that wasn't really there.

The only way you can really make love is if there was love to begin with—the forever kind of love, forsaking all others.

∽◦◦∾

Chastity, then, isn't only for the unmarried. It's a lifelong discipline. Within marriage, it enables us to experience the fullness of spousal union. But that's not a message you're going to hear on most television shows, or read in *Cosmo*—and it's certainly not the one that many teenagers are getting in school. In a classroom culture that discourages public expressions of faith, teenagers are instead taught—in sex-ed curricula developed by organizations such as Planned Parenthood—that hormones are destiny.

For several years, Planned Parenthood and its allies have been waging a campaign against abstinence education, because they believe it is cruel to expect youths to overcome their urges. Instead, they treat teens as though they are automatons, unable to make moral decisions for themselves.

In this bizarre alternate universe—which, sadly, has become reality for many of today's youth—good and evil themselves are redefined. No longer is it bad to allow oneself to use and be used sexually. The only sin is failing to "protect" yourself by using a condom or another form of contraception.

Kids learn what they see in grown-ups—and today's adults are only too glad to abdicate moral responsibility. Doris Day's celebrated chastity was the fruit of thousands of years of Judeo-Christian tradition. Once faith lost its place in modern culture—as it did during the mid-1960s, when the cover of *Time* asked, "Is God Dead?"—the concept of chastity became worse than irrelevant. It was unfathomable.

But chastity didn't disappear. Like the early Christians in the Roman catacombs, it went underground. Today, as the fruits of the sexual revolution prove to be loneliness, divorce, and disease, chastity is not only back—it's the *new* revolution. So out, it's in.

Being chaste is a bold challenge to modern culture, because it proves that people are not automatons but human beings with free will, able to control who and what they are.

The symbol of early Christians was a fish—perhaps from Jesus's saying He would make His disciples "fishers of men" (Matthew 4:19 NKJV)—and, like the salmon swimming upstream, we're charged to go against the flow. I battle the current, because it's the only right way to use the abundant life that has been given to me. As G. K. Chesterton wrote, "A dead thing can go with the stream, but only a living thing can go against it."[5]

There's a Monty Python sketch that depicts the World War II–era British army using a "killer joke" against the Germans—a joke that literally destroys everyone who hears it. I think of faith as being the opposite: a joke that, when you're in on it, makes you alive, while everyone who's not in on it decays.

What is a joke, after all, but something that makes you smile—at least the first time you hear it? It's like a sweet fragrance, as the apostle Paul wrote: "For we are to God the fragrance of Christ among those who are being saved and among those who are perishing. To the one we are the aroma of death leading to death, and to the other the aroma of life leading to life" (2 Corinthians 2:15–16 NKJV).

In other words, some people get it—and some don't. Faith, like humor, is all about having a sense of the absurd—and feeling deep inside that the people who puff themselves up are the very people who need to come down a notch or three. *Especially* if that "people" is one's self.

A century ago, the *Times of London*, after publishing a series of articles titled "What's Wrong with the World?" received this letter:

Dear Sir: Regarding your article "What's Wrong with the World?" I am. Yours truly,

G. K. CHESTERTON[6]

To some of my friends, when I talk about my faith, I'm like the boor at parties who keeps repeating the same tired and offensive joke. I wish they would understand that as sanctimonious as I may seem, the truth is, not only am I in on the joke, but, like Chesterton, I'm the punch line as well.

The funny thing is, now that I understand the meaning of the humor, I wouldn't have it any other way.

Chesterton wrote in *Orthodoxy* that he suspected "[t]here was something that [Jesus] hid from all men when He went up a mountain to pray.

"There was something that He covered constantly by abrupt silence or impetuous isolation," Chesterton went on. "There was some one thing that was too great for God to show us when He walked upon our earth; and I have sometimes fancied that it was His mirth."

three
becoming a singular sensation

A New York City university recently offered continuing-education students a course on "Living Single."

"Now, more than at any other time, the single lifestyle is viewed as a viable, desirable choice for men and women," read the course description. "Whether they find themselves single again, or single still, many adults are not completely comfortable flying solo—or confident in their ability to do it successfully. Topics include: viewing the contemporary world; relating to couples; the dating scene, how to be part of it (or not); and battling the blues that sometimes arise. Enrich your life with resources on what to read, pursue, reflect on, and talk about to gain confidence with single living."

As a final note, the description added, "No grades are given for this course."

Phew! What a relief. After getting your certificate in "Living Single," wouldn't you hate to have to confess to some guy you met in a bar that you got a C-minus in "viewing the contemporary world"?

Seriously, as I read that course description touting "the single lifestyle," it all seems to boil down to a single word: *lack*.

The paradigm for modern singlehood is yin without yang. The modern single woman's goal is to relate to men from a single perspective, and to have fulfilling relationships with them without ever becoming part of anything larger than herself. As my parents' generation would have said, she is on her own trip.

For a woman harboring the least bit of longing for something deeper, this modern-singlehood rut ultimately devolves into the familiar Bridget Jones merry-go-round, revolving around the hope that the ever-distant Darcy will come along one day and stop the music. I find the whole mind-set terribly stifling, and I think most other single women do too—they certainly complain about it enough. Yet, most seem helpless to find an alternative.

The truth is that there is another way, but most women don't want to think about it. It's scary to get off the merry-go-round while it's still spinning. Sometimes, however, it's the only way to get off a ride to nowhere.

A woman with the courage to step out into the unknown, risking temporary loneliness for a shot at lasting joy, is more than a "single." She's *singular.* Instead of defining herself by what she lacks—a relationship with a man—she defines herself by what she has: a relationship with God.

A single woman bases her actions on how they will or won't affect her single, lacking state. She goes to parties based on whether or not there will be new men to meet—if there won't, then the food and drink had better be first rate. She chooses female friends who likewise define themselves as single and lacking, thus reinforcing her own cynicism.

But a singular woman bases her actions on how they will enable her to be the person she believes God wants her to be. If she longs to be married, she trusts that God has a plan for her and that a husband is part of that plan. Moreover, she trusts that God will provide all that He has planned for her if she follows His will for her life, making the best use of the gifts she has been given. She'll still enjoy parties and meeting people—but as ends in and of themselves, not just as a means of finding a man.

A single woman, in seeking a husband, feels the need to act in a coy, sly, or deceptive manner—even if she normally would never think of intentionally misleading someone. Somehow, to be cagey to a man within the parameters of a budding relationship doesn't seem wrong to her. Likewise, she accepts a level of superficiality from a man she's dating that she wouldn't tolerate from her friends. She's not stupid—she just loses perspective when facing the possibility of a relationship. Her brain compartmentalizes dating into its own relative morality—"all's fair in love and war."

A singular woman behaves with an honesty and lack of guile that will appear arresting to the love interest who expects a superficial relationship—as well it should. With her words and actions, she is speaking a deeper language, one that can be understood only by the kind of man for whom she longs—one of integrity. Such a man will understand that the singular woman's straightforwardness and absence of pretense is rooted in deep respect for him as a fellow child of God. For example, Miss Singular is not going to suggest to her love interest that he faces competition for her if no such competition exists. She expects him to be equally truthful in return.

Perhaps the most noticeable difference between a single woman and a singular woman is one of gratitude. Because the single woman defines herself by her lack, she is plagued with a sense of sadness and resentment at what she doesn't have. When positive things happen in her life, she may be thankful, but she may just as well respond with a sense of entitlement—"At last, I'm getting what everyone else has."

The singular woman not only expresses more gratitude than the single woman, but she also expresses it for different things. She's not just grateful for things she receives but for the opportunities she has to *give*. She knows in her heart the spirit of G. K. Chesterton's words: "The world will never starve for want of wonders; but only for want of wonder."[7]

Being single places you in a mind-set where you are measured by what you do, whether good or bad—how well you are able to attract men, acquire friends, make money, say witty things, and put forth other social commodities. Ultimately, your capacity in these areas is finite; you can do only so much before you've exhausted your resources. The world may say you can never be too rich or too thin, but all it takes is a look at celebrities' love lives to see that wealth and slenderness don't guarantee happiness. (That's not to say I wouldn't be very happy to squeeze into the size 6 silver 1960s-style minidress I bought for forty-five dollars on what turned out to be the only day of my life that I ever weighed under 115 pounds.)

To be singular is to embark on a wide excursion of discovery. No more is your identity limited to qualities that can be defined by the checkoff boxes in an online personal ad. It's no longer what you do—but who you are. Prayerfully, you strive to develop inner qualities—like empathy, patience, humility, and faith in spite of hardship.

Such a transition is not easy, especially when your temptation around an attractive man is to shift back into your single self. There's a comforting familiarity in interacting with others on a superficial level and knowing that they will interact with you in the same way. But I can tell you from experience that the more you develop a singular identity, the more confident you will become around men and in every area of your life, because you will be comfortable in your own skin.

I spent many years of my life being single. I have nothing to show for it except the ability to toss my hair fetchingly and a mental catalog of a thousand banal things to say to fill the awkward, unbearably lonely moments between having sex and putting my clothes back on. You never see those moments in TV or movies, because they strike to the heart of the black hole that casual sex can never fill.

Now that I'm singular, I understand why the popular culture tries so relentlessly to define single women as superficial and libidinous singles rather than deep singulars who value marriage enough to hold out for it. To be singular is to understand the meaning of chastity, and chastity by its very nature goes against the popular culture's beliefs regarding sex and choice.

The culture tells unmarried women that it is perfectly normal and acceptable to act on our sexual desires—all the way. We only have to take the right precautions—physical ones, like using a condom—and we are "safe." What is abnormal, and even destructive, in the eyes of the culture, is to resist such desires, especially if we are doing so for moral reasons. The concept of deferring pleasure makes no sense in a consumer society where we are told we must take something when it's offered or risk its going off the market. We're told that even though men come and go like buses, the next one may not be such a good ride.

In light of such social prejudices, a singular woman is a revolutionary. Think about it: all it takes is one unmarried woman to live a dynamic, well-rounded, and happy life while avoiding premarital sex, and the culture's image of the drab spinster crumbles like a house of cards. That's why being singular is so exciting. It's an act of open rebellion—liberating you from an oppressive culture.

If there is one quality that marks our culture's conception of single-hood, it is hunger. A single woman who's up front about her desire to meet someone is seen as "man-hungry." If she's been looking for a while, she's viewed as "sex-starved" or "starved for affection."

The media would have you believe that the hunger of love may be satisfied as simply as the hunger for food. You find that for which you hunger—be it a bagel or a bachelor—indulge yourself, and then go on with your daily life until you get hungry again. But there is, in fact, a fundamental difference between the two desires.

Hunger for food points directly to the object that satisfies it. Despite our individual tastes, this hunger isn't divided into higher and lower forms. Whether we'd rather eat sushi or cottage cheese, the pangs are the same. If we eat enough of anything, we'll experience the feeling of being full.

Hunger for love points *beyond* the object that satisfies it.

If a married woman loves her husband, her desire to be loved in return is not fulfilled simply because her husband says he loves her. Nor is it fulfilled only because he treats her kindly or gives her presents. It's not even fulfilled just because, in addition to showing all manner of devotion, he has sex with her. We all know that a spouse can do all these things indefinitely, and not be in love.

The love between husband and wife, as with all types of love, is fulfilled only when both partners together look beyond externals and discover that something they can't describe binds them together. That something, I believe, is God's own love, and it may truly be called a taste of heaven. It is the food for which we hunger most, even when our desires tell us that a longed-for mate holds the promise of satisfaction.

When Jesus saw a Samaritan woman approach the well where He was sitting and told her He could give her "living water," the woman thought at first that He was simply offering to quench her physical thirst.

I know how she felt. When you're used to being treated according to how useful you are—and treating others the same way—your expectations are lower. You also become less able to give of yourself, because you lose your perspective on what qualities are truly valuable—what Paul calls the "fruit of the Spirit" (Galatians 5:22 NKJV).

So, the Samaritan woman, thinking literally, said, "Sir, give me this water" (John 4:15 NKJV).

Jesus's response came out of left field: "Go, call your husband, and come here" (4:16 NKJV).

When the woman answered that she had no husband, Jesus said to her, "You have well said, 'I have no husband,' for you have had five husbands, and the one whom you now have is not your husband; in that you spoke truly" (4:17–18 NKJV).

Note what Jesus was doing in that instance—and what He *wasn't* doing.

He effortlessly shifted the topic from the woman's physical needs to what was really troubling her—her spiritual needs. She hungered for something that five husbands and a live-in boyfriend could not fulfill.

Yet, Jesus didn't pass judgment on the woman. Instead, He held a mirror up to her conscience. The realization made her run to the nearby city, telling the people, "Come, see a Man who told me all things that I ever did" (4:29 NKJV).

Jesus didn't really tell her all things she had done. He enabled her to see clearly, for the first time, her life and her longings. The truth cut her to the heart. She was able to understand that truth because she herself was truthful—admitting to Jesus that something was missing from her life.

If you want to receive the love for which you hunger, the first step is to admit to yourself that you have that hunger, with everything it entails—weakness, vulnerability, the feeling of an empty space inside. To tell yourself simply, "I'll be happy once I have a boyfriend," is to deny the depth and seriousness of your longing. It turns the hunger into a superficial desire for flesh and blood when what we really want is someone to share divine love with us—to be for us God with skin on.

Psalm 107 tells what God has in store for those who have this spiritual hunger:

He turns a wilderness into pools of water,
And the watersprings into dry ground.
There He makes the hungry dwell,
That they may establish a city for a dwelling place. (vv. 35–36 NKJV)

What does this tell us?

You could say that it means God will feed us. But there's a deeper message: to live in the city of God, *you must be hungry.*

It doesn't say, "God takes the satisfied people and sets them up so they can stay satisfied." It says, "There He makes the hungry dwell . . ."

The psalmist is referring to the same hunger felt by the Samaritan woman who asked Jesus for the living water, and the same longing that Jesus speaks of in the Sermon on the Mount, when He blesses "they which do hunger and thirst after righteousness" (Matthew 5:6 KJV). By hungering and thirsting after righteousness, Jesus means not merely longing to do right, but longing to exist in a right state with God. It's the deep-seated desire to align one's heart with His so that, in one's love for Him and one another, one can become like Him.

When you are hungry, really hungry, it's hard to think about anything else. Likewise, hungering for righteousness means not being able to rest until your hunger is satisfied. As Augustine wrote of God, "Our hearts are restless until we find rest in You."[8]

A reporter once asked one of Hollywood's greatest beauties her secret to keeping her weight down. Her answer was not what the dieters of this world had been waiting for. She said she ate small portions, never allowing herself to get full. Always, she said, she left the dining table a little hungry.

When I first read that story, I thought sarcastically, *Well, good for her*. I was and am determined to leave the dining table full even if it means loading up on breadsticks.

But when it comes to spiritual hunger, we are all Sophia Loren.

Our citizenship is in heaven. We are not meant to be fully satisfied on this earth. Thankfully, there are things we can do in this life to draw closer to the spiritual food that will fill us in the world to come. We can even taste it.

Here's an exercise you can practice today. Whenever you feel hungry or thirsty, before you fulfill that need, get in touch with it and try to grasp—just for a moment—how dependent you are on God for everything in your life. Make friends with that sense of longing, and it will change your whole way of life.

Hunger—real spiritual hunger—is a gift. Cherish it.

the agony and the ecstasy: countering the culture

Walking to the train station after work one night, I passed by a bus-shelter ad touting a British sitcom, *Coupling*, with the slogan, "Love, lust, and everything in between."

I was struck by the bizarreness of the slogan. Then it hit me: there is *nothing* in between love and lust.

I don't mean that the two are the same. I mean that they're not on the same continuum.

Try to substitute those nouns with others equally disparate and you'll see what I mean. "Hatred, head colds, and everything in between." "Irony, iron deficiency, and everything in between." It's ludicrous.

Admittedly, it is possible to confuse lust with love—just as it's possible to think that the world is against you when you've really just forgotten to have your first cup of coffee. Remember the exchange in Dickens's *A Christmas Carol* between Marley's ghost and an incredulous Scrooge:

"Why do you doubt your senses?"

"Because," said Scrooge, "a little thing affects them. A slight disorder of the stomach makes them cheats. You may be an undigested bit of beef, a blot of mustard, a crumb of cheese, a fragment of an underdone potato. There's more of gravy than of grave about you, whatever you are!"

It's the same thing with our sexual appetite as it is with our appetite for food. A handsome face may awaken the undigested ghost of an ex-boyfriend. But the feeling isn't comparable to love—neither in kind, nor in degree.

Yet, our culture—both in the media and in everyday interactions—relentlessly puts forth the idea that lust is a way station on the road to love. Make that more than a way station: it's more like an indefinite layover.

This misguided, hedonistic philosophy harms both men and women, but is particularly damaging to women, as it pressures them to subvert their deepest emotional desires. Women are built for bonding. We are vessels, and we seek to be filled. For that reason, sex will always leave us feeling empty unless we are certain that we are loved.

When I was having casual sex, there was one moment I dreaded more than any other. I dreaded it not out of fear that the sex would be bad, but out of fear that it would be *good*.

If the sex was good, then, even if I knew in my heart that the relationship wouldn't work, I would still feel as though the act had bonded me with my sex partner in a deeper way than we had been bonded before. It's in the nature of sex to awaken deep emotions within us—emotions that are distinctly unwelcome when one is trying to keep it light.

At such times, the worst moment was when it was all over.

Suddenly, I was jarred back to earth. Then I'd lie back and feel . . .

. . . bereft.

My partner was still there, and if I was really lucky, he'd lie down next to me. Yet, I couldn't help feeling like the spell had been broken. We could nuzzle or giggle, or we could fall asleep in each other's arms, but I knew it was playacting—and so did my partner. We weren't really intimate—it had just been a game. The circus had left town.

Sex and the City heroine Carrie Bradshaw once asked, "Can a woman have sex like a man?" The question's not new. Helen Gurley Brown posed it nearly forty years earlier in *Sex and the Single Girl*—and answered yes: "Like a man, [a woman] is a sexual creature."

But unlike a man, a woman's body has to allow her lover inside—to let him literally get under her skin—and that will always frustrate her quest for quasi-masculine, no-strings sex.

I realize that I don't have to convince you ladies of this. You've already read the blurbs on the back cover of this book—maybe even cheated and skipped to the last page (shame on you). But even if you know in your heart that you've been hurt by crossing physical boundaries with a date, it's important to realize that the pain was not because—as *Cosmo* would claim—you were doing it wrong. It's because you were doing it *right*. It's the situation—seeking physical excitement with a man for its own sake, outside the love and security of a marital relationship—that was wrong.

Much of the popular culture, particularly magazines directed at single women, hold up "having sex like a man" as a goal toward which all intelligent women should strive. Women who refuse to hold to that ideal are derided as provincial, hopelessly backward prudes. In the face of such social pressure, it's no wonder, then, that some of the most brilliant, dynamic women have succumbed to the idea that they have to perfect the art of casual sex.

At base, the arbiters of hipness are cynical. They know in their tin hearts that casual sex doesn't make women happy—that's why they feel the need to continually promote it. As a result, daily life for those who dare to resist the culture's temptations is filled with reminders that they are in this world but not of it.

The strains of constant conflict with an unsympathetic culture were painfully familiar to the faithful during the early years of the church. Paul described it in his letter to the Philippians: "For to you it has been granted on behalf of Christ, not only to believe in Him, but also to suffer for His sake, having the same conflict which you saw in me and now hear is in me" (1:29–30 NKJV).

But it's more than mere conflict. The word Paul uses that the King James Bible translates as "conflict" is really *agon*—Greek for "agony."

The word *agon* appears several times in Paul's letters. Each time, it refers to an earthly conflict that requires faith to overcome—an ongoing battle that we will fight as long as we are in this mortal coil.

"Agony" doesn't mean sudden, sharp bursts of pain, but rather a long, drawn-out ordeal. That makes it a fitting term to describe the ongoing battle faced by those who strive to align their own wills with God's will for them.

The most challenging part of chastity isn't overcoming temptations. It's gaining the spiritual resources to joyfully face day-to-day life as a cultural outsider. It's a conflict between pleasing men and pleasing God. This is the "good fight of faith" that Paul describes in both 1 Timothy 6:12 and 2 Timothy 4:7 (NKJV)—and it's no coincidence that the word he used for "fight" in both cases was *agon*.

There must be a reason why people, in the face of loneliness and isolation, are willing to forgo easy pleasures in hope of better ones. For me, it's because I became convinced that having premarital sex—contrary to what our culture claims—actually made me less likely to gain a husband. Moreover, I realized that my readiness to engage in physical intimacy altered me emotionally to the point that I was not equipped to sustain a marriage.

Jesus endured the Cross, "for the joy that was set before Him" (Hebrews 12:2 NKJV).

I can't always see the joy that is set before me.

But I know one thing.

Where my old way of life is concerned, there is *no* joy behind me.

There's nothing about my way of life before I became chaste that I could possibly revisit and be happy. If there is joy—and I do believe there is; otherwise, I wouldn't be alive today—then it's got to be ahead.

∽∾

Before, when I sought sexual experiences with men, it was as a distraction from the emptiness I felt inside.

The emptiness was self-defeating, I knew. I wanted desperately to love and be loved by one man, but I couldn't really imagine why anyone would love me. As a result, I was caught in the downward spiral of the addict, seeking to fill the empty space with meaningless sexual experiences that I knew would leave me emptier than before.

When I shared my insecurities with family and friends, they all offered me the same advice I could find in every self-help book and women's magazine: "Just believe in yourself."

They would list my attractive qualities and tell me to count my blessings. I was only going through a hard time, they said. Things would get better. All I had to do was believe in myself.

And so, I would believe in myself—until the next disappointment came along. Then I'd feel like an even bigger failure.

Life had wounded me. I felt oppressed, impotent, and painfully aware that there was nothing I could do to heal myself.

I was absolutely right.

My problem lay in how I perceived my own weakness. I was acutely aware of it, longing with all my heart to be rid of it—and didn't realize that the answer was right in front of me.

The emptiness that I perceived as a black hole was really what Christians call a God-shaped vacuum. The fact that I was aware of it, as painful as it was, actually put me at an advantage. Unlike those who engage in self-destructive behavior without any inkling of the consequences of their actions, I knew that there was no future in my in-the-moment lifestyle.

My mistake was in doing what I was told to do—believing in myself.

"Actors who can't act believe in themselves; and debtors who won't pay," writes G. K. Chesterton in *Orthodoxy*. "It would be much truer to say that a man will certainly fail, because he *believes in himself*. Complete self-confidence is not merely a sin; complete self-confidence is a weakness."

Indeed, just when I thought I was at my strongest—the times when I most believed I had the self-confidence to face life as a single young woman, with all its possibilities and pitfalls—I was weakest.

The reason for my weakness may be found in Chesterton's examples of self-confident individuals. Actors who can't act. Debtors who can't pay. People whose existence depends on putting forth a front without the resources to back it up. The very nature of self-confidence is that it springs from within. It can't be put on. Put another way, you can't transform a pair of $14.99 Fayva slingbacks into a pair of $600 Manolo stilettos with a mere coat of paint.

Even at my lowest point, I had the grace that God gives to all—the "treasure in earthen vessels" (2 Corinthians 4:7 NKJV). But in my darkness, I cared only about how men who didn't know what was really inside me assessed this treasure—not the value it would hold to a truly loving man someday. And I had no concept whatsoever of the value it held in the eyes of God.

∽◌℘

What was it that Holden Caulfield said in J. D. Salinger's *The Catcher in the Rye* about the movies messing everybody up? It's so true. I used to watch romantic male leads in old films—like fiery Orson Welles in *Jane Eyre*, giving that speech where he envisioned a string under his left ribs, "tightly and inextricably knotted to a similar string in the corresponding quarter" of Jane's little frame—and my chest would swell as I'd imagine the character saying those passionate words to me.

But while the actors were real, the characters they portrayed existed only in my imagination, where my fantasies could fill in the missing facets of their personalities. And I knew, ultimately, that such fantasies were misleading, because however I tried to make them realistic, I couldn't.

It was easy to extend my practice of filling in personalities with fantasy to my relationships with real-life love interests. Each one would have some qualities that neared the ones I'd idealized, so I would focus on those, painting them brighter with the colors of imagination. It was a game, and I believed everyone did it.

They did it to me too. Men would approach me because they saw something in me that matched a fantasy they had. If they matched some aspect of my fantasy, I would in turn try to make myself more like the fantasy they had of me—be it witty, worldly, or worshipful.

I knew that the right man would love me as I was, and yet I could not imagine being loved that way from day one. I thought that relationships in the twenty-first century began with becoming attracted to one's image of a person, and deepened into love as one discovered that the real person was not so much different from the image one had developed.

My understanding of love—along with the rest of my life— changed dramatically at age thirty-one, when I received faith in God for the first time. At once, I was healed of my bitter loneliness, and I saw what my freewheeling lifestyle was doing to my spirit.

Now that I'm living chastely, striving with all my heart to see those around me as individuals and not as objects or stereotypes, I believe for the first time that I am growing capable of loving fully.

I know that when I meet my future husband, I will be changed. But unlike past relationships, I won't be changing to fit a fantasy. It will be more like what C. S. Lewis describes in *Mere Christianity*, when he tells the story of a man who was made to wear a mask that made him look much more attractive than he really was. One day, after wearing it for years, he was finally able to take it off—and found that his own face had grown to fit it.

"He was now really beautiful," Lewis writes. "What had begun as disguise had become a reality."

When I meet my future husband, I know there is something I will have to do before I can reciprocate his love: I will have to accept that I am beloved. It will require donning a mask of sorts, because it won't come automatically or naturally, although I'm sure my emotions will quickly grow to fit it.

As I write this, I am searching—just for contrast—for a relevant quote from the single woman's gospel of our age: the wit and wisdom of Carrie Bradshaw. What comes up is this aphorism: "The most exciting, challenging and significant relationship of all is the one you have with yourself. And if you can find someone to love the you you love, well, that's just fabulous."[9]

I've had an exciting, challenging, and significant relationship with myself for more than three decades. It's not hard for me to find someone to love the me I love. What I never imagined before I was chaste was that I could hope to find someone to love the me I *don't* love. My weaknesses, my insecurities, my shortcomings, all the times I miss the mark.

Through changing the way I perceive myself and the world, looking beyond appearances, I'm finally beginning to gain a real understanding of love beyond old movies and what Joni Mitchell called "the dizzy dancing way you feel." I now realize that all that time I thought I was romanticizing love in my mind, I was really limiting it. What seemed like cockeyed optimism was actually coarse cynicism.

That's why at this time of my life—when the world tells me that I'm farther from marriage than ever, with no current "prospects"— I am, against all odds, hopelessly . . . hopeful.

I may have many more nights of walking down lonely streets and being mocked by bus-shelter ads. But I believe that the only real "in between" isn't between lust and love. It's between this world and the kingdom of God. And I have to pray for patience so that running the race across that divide, however exhausting, is worth the *agon*.

Thankfully, Someone has already blazed a trail for me.

the first cut is the deepest

Romantics call the warm, fuzzy feeling one experiences after having sex an "afterglow." When you're not married, it can feel more like an aftermath.

Sometimes, after having sex with a man for the first time, I took advantage of the lingering illusion of intimacy by asking my bedmate something I wouldn't normally have the guts to ask.

"So . . . ," I'd say as I lay on my stomach, turning my head to speak as I propped myself up on my elbows. (You usually lie on your stomach after casual sex, because it feels too vulnerable to expose your naked body.)

". . . tell me about your first time."

Partly, I was simply trying to make conversation. Having just had sex with a man I didn't know all that well, I didn't want to scare him off by saying something deep. The most obvious thing to talk about after fornicating is . . . fornicating. But there was another reason, a subconscious reason why I posed the question.

I wanted to know what the man was like when he was vulnerable.

By the time I got to him, whether he was confident or insecure, he was already aware that he could get a woman into bed. What was he like before he knew how to slip into seduction mode and do the familiar dance? What was he like before he had developed a technique?

What, I wondered, was he like back when a woman could reach him in a way that no one had before?

I now realize that what I really wanted to know was not how my bedmate lost his virginity, but how he lost his innocence. The reason why the loss of innocence interested me was because I keenly felt the loss of my own.

$$\infty$$

Your loss of innocence is the defining point in your sexual history. It was the first time you crossed a certain boundary with a boy or a man who attracted you. It was the first time you took a step into the unknown—and discovered you could return from it alive. More than that, you realized you could go back, again and again.

You discovered that each time you recrossed that line, it felt less dangerous. If you wanted to recapture the thrill of dipping your toe into uncharted waters, you had to get in deeper.

Yet, as you explored further, you could never recapture that feeling you had before you took that first step—the feeling of hopefulness and unexplored possibilities. You might try to repeat the same thing you did before with a new man, but in your mind you would always compare your new date to those who had preceded him. Whether he was better, worse, or just different, he was coloring on pages that already contained the outlines of other men.

What exactly happened at that moment when you passed from innocence into worldliness? The simplest way to put it is that you realized for the first time that you could separate sexual sensation from love.

My brief relationship with my first "boyfriend"—that is, the first guy who lasted longer than a few yucky kisses—set the stage for my loss of innocence.

When I was fifteen and despairing of meeting a bright, hip guy at my New Jersey high school, my mom let me go on a weekend teen retreat at a Unitarian church. It was there that I met Gavin.

Gavin was hip, all right—a hard-core punk who was at home in the mosh pit—and also bright, with a sense of humor. He and a buddy founded a gang of pranksters that they called the UDL (Unitarian Defense League), a sort of "Clockwork Orange" for the suburban set. He was also cute, with his boyish, Johnny Ramone haircut, and would have been six feet tall if his smoker's slouch didn't take away two inches. Although he was just a year older than me, he seemed far more independent and experienced.

One night, after we had been dating about three weeks and had exchanged just a few quick kisses during that time, Gavin and I went to an all-ages punk concert in Lower Manhattan. I unfortunately proved to be a real drag, because I had yet to grasp that one does not go to a hard-core punk concert unless one is willing to get stomped on. In this case, it was Gavin's friend Rich who did the stomping—he jumped off the rafters and kicked my head on his way down. Perhaps the head kick was really meant as some sort of hard-core sign of camaraderie, but I took it very badly—running out of the nightclub, crying.

Gavin followed me out. He didn't say much to comfort me—it was obvious to him that I should have known what I was in for—but

I managed to stop crying. I had to leave soon anyway because my mom was going to pick me up, so he and I filled the rest of our time together with a walk around the block—a deserted area of warehouses and parking lots.

We stopped to lean against a metal barrier, and he started kissing me. I was very self-conscious because I'd only kissed a couple of boys before, and those were boys who didn't know what they were doing. From the way Gavin kissed, I could tell that he did know what he was doing, and I wasn't sure how to handle this new stage of our relationship.

Back then, I didn't believe in waiting until marriage to have sex. I grew up in a liberal household; neither of my parents wanted to seem like prudes. It was understood that I would have sex when I was ready—whether married or not. But I did have from childhood a deep desire to wait to have sex until I was really and truly "in love"—whatever that meant.

I don't recall telling Gavin that I wanted to wait to have sex until I was really in love, but he must have picked up on it. At least, that was my guess when I thought afterward about what transpired between us on that dark street. All I knew was that after I got into my mom's car, I never saw him again. He stopped calling me and stopped returning my calls. The message I took out of it was that I had moved too slowly for him; he was experienced, after all.

As the months went by and I kept rehashing my few dates with Gavin in my head, the message was clear: even if I was going to save sex for when I was finally in love, I had to get more experience. I would show my dream man that I wasn't uptight. It was the only way to keep him interested until the magic moment when everything would fall into place.

In the fall of my senior year of high school, when I was sixteen (having skipped a year in my haste to graduate), I hopped a train to visit a man I'll call Travis, at his East Village apartment.

Travis was a magazine writer and record-label employee originally from Nebraska—and twice my age. Two years earlier, I had phoned the editor of an underground pop-culture magazine for which he wrote. I was fascinated with entertainment journalism and brazenly asked the editor if he would meet my friends and me for lunch sometime. The editor—no doubt bemused to get a phone call from a fourteen-year-old girl in New Jersey—did meet us, and he brought Travis along.

I don't know what sparked my visit to Travis on that day two years after our meeting, or why it took me so long to make the trip. Since our lunch, we had kept up with each other through occasional letters. I was impressed that a man I considered important took an interest in me. To me, there was nothing cooler than working for a major label and writing magazine articles about hip music and movies. I was terribly eager to learn about all the important things I'd missed living out in suburbia, and I wanted to learn from Travis.

He also had another side that I found intriguing, in an edgy kind of way. He made a side income writing for pornographic magazines, including *Screw* and *Penthouse Letters*.

I wasn't a fan of pornography and knew there were good feminist reasons to oppose it. Walking east from the PATH station to Travis's place, I passed the woman from Feminists Fighting Pornography who stood every Saturday at a table at Broadway and Eighth Street, shouting in her thick New York accent, *"Women! Foight back!* Soign the *petition!"* Beside her was a giant blowup of the notorious cover of *Hustler* that showed a woman's legs sticking out of a meat grinder.

Despite my reservations, the idea that Travis was involved with the pornography industry gave his corn-fed Nebraskan demeanor an air of danger. It added to the pleasant sense of rebelliousness that I already felt going into New York City by myself to see a much older man.

∽∾

The only place to sit in Travis's studio apartment was his king-size bed. We hung out for a while and brought each other up to speed on what had happened in our lives since the one time we'd met. I told him I'd seen a video by a singer he'd helped get onto the label he worked for. Finally—and I must have known this would happen—he asked if he could kiss me.

I knew for certain that I was attracted to men. More than that, I was capable of being overwhelmingly attracted, with a crush so intense that it virtually blinded me and made me swoon.

I did not feel that way with Travis. But neither was I repelled by him.

He was . . . *there*. Pleasant looking. There was nothing particularly unattractive about him. And that, combined with my lack of a crush on him, made him safe.

Ever since Gavin had dumped me, I'd felt as though I couldn't get arrested. Looking at photos of myself from that time, I see that I wasn't unattractive, but at the time I was convinced that I was chubby and plain. None of the boys I liked at school would have anything to do with me. There seemed to be some sort of "it" factor that I lacked.

Travis fed my ego when I was at my most vulnerable. If he found me attractive, chances were that someone else—someone I'd be crazy about—would too. In the meantime, I thought, I could gain some experience with him, so that boys I liked would no longer see me as goofy or—worse—uptight.

But first came the uncertain moment when I told Travis that I was a virgin—and what's more, planned to stay that way.

He assured me that he just wanted to "neck." Anytime I wanted, I could just turn on the red lights.

I agreed. Travis went to his LP collection and pulled out an album from his youth, the Flamin' Groovies' *Teenage Head*. He adored the idea of making out like a teenager.

∞

I visited Travis several more times that school year. During that time, neither of us ever removed each other's clothing or touched each other under clothes. I was too quick with the red lights for that—and he would always stop, as he had promised.

Not feeling any hormonal rush during my sessions with Travis, I viewed the experiences as an opportunity to learn what a man experiences when he's excited. I remember noticing how his breathing rate changed and his neck would heat up. It gave me an egotistical pleasure to see how a touch or kiss from me would excite him. Only my body was really with him; my mind was watching the scene as if it was a TV show, while my emotions were buried too deeply for me to realize how they were being affected.

I told my mom that I was friends with Travis—I had a hard time hiding anything from her, because we were close—but I didn't tell her we were more than friends. She later told me that she knew, but she didn't push it. A new Christian, she was just starting to walk the walk at that time. While she was concerned for me, I think she was uncomfortable at the thought of dictating chastity.

I had mixed feelings about what Travis and I were doing. On the one hand, it gave me something exciting to tell the girls I lunched with at my high-school cafeteria, who listened with interest even though they thought the idea of dating a thirty-two-year-old was kind of weird. On the other, it got to be boring after a while. I knew Travis wasn't the one, and it was pointless to take things farther. But I also liked the feeling of being a grown-up: getting away for a secret rendezvous at a real New York City apartment—not just some-body's parents' basement—and having a bit of suspense over how far things might go.

⤜∽◇∽⤛

By the spring semester of my freshman year of college, when I was seventeen, I had long since moved on from Travis, but we were still friendly. He invited me to a party celebrating the release of a book by an underground cartoonist.

At the party, Travis greeted me warmly. He wanted me to meet the publisher of the marijuana-lovers' magazine *High Times*. I wasn't into drugs, but when it came to meeting downtown hipsters, I wasn't picky.

As Travis brought me over to the publisher, he said, "Is it okay if I tell him about us? About how you used to come over, and we'd make out, and because you were a virgin, you'd put on the red lights?"

For a moment, I was thrown off guard, but I eventually told him it was okay.

I never hated Travis for what he did to me. In his and my situa-tional ethics of the time, he was a model of honesty and respect. But I think of what it meant to him, to be this jaded pornography writer getting an ego boost from telling people about his experience with a virgin, and it seems terribly sad. No, not sad—make that pathetic.

And the most pathetic part is, I let him do it. That was how far gone I was. I had lost my innocence—and I wasn't even aware that I had lost it, or that there had been anything to lose.

∽∾

There are certain points in one's memory where time seems to stop. They're like fault lines—a nexus between past and present—and one keeps returning to them. As I look back on when I was sexually active, I keep returning to those afternoons with Travis. Not because they were sexually exciting—they weren't. Compared to experiences I had later, the Travis sessions were about two notches above a trip to the dentist.

No, the experiences in that studio apartment on First Avenue stick in my mind because they represent a contradiction that is essential to nonmarital sex. It's something that I don't think the purveyors of a "sex-positive" culture will ever understand. (I think sex within marriage *is* positive, but I'm referring to the views of those who take it outside that context.)

From the sex-positive perspective, the Travis sessions were perfect "outercourse," as safe as safe could be. Save for saliva, no bodily fluids were exchanged. There was no genital contact.

However, from a Christian perspective, I was doing the absolute worst thing I could possibly do to my soul. It was, truly, unsafe sex. In a way, it was worse for me even than if I were actually having intercourse, because if I were doing so—as bad as that would have been for me—there would have been more of a chance that I'd realize what was going on.

As it was, I was like the person who takes a little poison each day and eventually becomes immune. Poison is never good for you; having the ability to ingest it without dying isn't a reason to do so on a regular basis.

In my case, I was learning to detach, to feel as though I could separate the physical actions of sex from its emotional consequences. I was also learning to be vicarious—to treat my partner as an object, to the point where my enjoyment consisted in seeing the effect I was having on him. It was a feeling of control, and it enabled me to further detach, so that I could move my partner without being moved myself.

My goal in all this was to have the excitement, ego boost, and physical companionship of sex—however temporary—without getting hurt. I always knew the separation would come and I'd be alone again. If I could limit how close I was to my partner in the first place, then the separation wouldn't be as pronounced, and I wouldn't crash.

∽◇◇◇∾

You lose your innocence when you learn to detach. You detach in order to protect yourself. You protect yourself, and sex goes from being a shared, outer-directed experience of love to an insular, narcissistic experience of insecurity.

The answer is to stop protecting yourself, and the only way to do that is to take yourself out of situations where you have to protect yourself. To truly connect with someone, you must allow yourself to be vulnerable. You can't be vulnerable if you're always having to ask yourself whether the man you desire will be there to catch you when you fall.

I know that I will never regain my innocence. But I *can* regain my vulnerability.

six

why it's easy to blame mom and dad (and why you shouldn't)

We usually think of a legacy as something one leaves after one dies, but there are some ways that parents can leave a legacy while they are still alive. If your parents are like mine, you've already received a legacy that's in no way welcome. It's the legacy of divorce.

Looking at the big picture, I know my parents were only trying to do what they sincerely believed was best for them and for my sister and me. But that doesn't take away the fact that their failure to stay together harmed my own chances of having a lasting marriage. Many studies show that women whose parents divorced are more likely to become divorced themselves.

If your parents divorced, or if they remained together but were unhappy, there are two ways you can view your family history in relation to who you are now. You can hold it up as an excuse for whatever prevents you from entering and sustaining a healthy relationship. Or you can use your insight to divorce yourself from your damaged perspective of love and marriage.

You can guess which option I prefer—but it wasn't always that way.

⤜⤛

My parents separated when I was five and divorced when I was six. My mother was given custody of my older sister and me, and my dad had visitation on weekends. Like many Seventies parents, they were intent on having a "good" divorce. They believed that if they did not fight over custody and if they treated each other with grudging respect, my sister and I would make it through the breakup with only a minimum of emotional damage.

The truth was that they both retained hurt feelings toward each other, which neither of them could hide. I learned early on that Mom thought Dad was superficial—after all, he remarried the year after their split—and Dad thought Mom was flighty. It also hurt me that Mom would harp about the times when Dad slighted me in some way—like when he'd missed my school recitals—while Dad would notice if Mom was dressing me in shabby clothes. (Of course, Mom had a ready response to that: Dad should use his superior paycheck to buy new duds for me.)

Those negative opinions that each parent expressed about the other sank into me, giving me preconceptions about Mom and Dad that I had to later work to overcome. But the most profound effect of my parents' putting me inside their own emotional drama was that they made me prematurely aware of grown-up dysfunction. Without meaning to do so, they created a pint-size cynic.

⤜⤛

Unlike many children of divorce, I had a father who made some effort to stay in my life—at least at first. Some of my earliest memories are of him taking me fishing, swimming with me in his pool, and secretly burying coins at the beach and then hinting where I might find treasure.

When I was seven, Dad remarried and I saw much less of him. My sister and I still saw him on weekends—really only from Saturday morning through Sunday morning—but he and my step-mother would often go out on Saturday night. It was the only night they could have to themselves, they said. That might well make sense to a grown-up, but it made no sense to me as a kid.

When I did see my father, I had less and less to talk about with him. I was used to being around my mom, who was keenly inter-ested in the details of my life at school, my friends, and my hobbies. Dad couldn't relate to me as easily; he just wanted to know that I was getting good grades and was staying out of trouble. It seemed that while my mother loved me for who I was, Dad loved me only for what I did.

I felt that I had to earn my father's affection. It was a limited and precious commodity, but I knew it was there. I strained for it, but all too often it was just out of reach.

∞

My earliest attitudes about sex were shaped from what I saw in the lives of my sister and especially my mother. I learned from them that a woman can be highly intelligent and beautiful, and yet have a tremendously difficult time meeting a responsible, gentlemanly man who wishes to be married for life. (Eventually, they both did meet and marry such men, but not until well after I'd reached adulthood.)

When I was twelve, I became the only child left at home, as my sister went off to college. With my sister absent, and myself my mother's closest confidante, I gained a disturbingly close perspective on the poignancy of Mom's dating life. Ours was a postfeminist lifestyle in the vein of the then-popular sitcom *One Day at a Time*, where Mom would run me by each new boyfriend to ensure that he was comfortable with the fact that she had a kid. It was my job to be tolerant and open to the possibility that this man might turn out to be Mom's Mr. Right.

In the best of circumstances, it's hard for the daughter of a single mother to acclimate herself to her mother's search for a husband. When that search brings forth men who treat the mom as a mere way station between relationships—it's just devastating.

This was the seventies and early eighties, the age of SNAGs— Sensitive New Age Guys. They really were snags too. My mother attracted them because she was New Age herself, doing kundalini yoga and attending lectures by various gurus. They were ethical and they treated her with what passed for respect in the singles world, but they seemed unable to give of themselves. Certainly, they never saw the beauty that I saw in my mother. Since my relationship with my father was distant, I wondered if there were any men capable of seeing and appreciating inner beauty.

In both her search for a husband and her search for a fulfilling spirituality, Mom was, in my eyes, fueled by a longing to fill the empty space—what I would now call the proverbial God-shaped vacuum. As I hit my teens, I felt the vacuum too, and I likewise longed for male companionship. But I was determined not to be hurt the way I had seen my mother hurt. Having premarital sex seemed like a surefire way to get burned. So I decided early on that I would not have sex until . . . marriage? That would be great. However, I didn't think I could wait until then. Instead, I resolved that I would wait to have sex until I was really "in love."

The problem was—and I was well aware of this—I didn't know the first thing about what a healthy love relationship was like—how it began or how it was sustained. Sex, then, became a symbol of a feeling that was unattainable. If I thought I was in love and had sex, and then it turned out that the feeling really wasn't love, what was left?

The solution, I believed, was to put sex off for as long as possible, until I was absolutely sure that it was worth the risk of disappointment.

It was a bold plan—and doomed for failure.

Although I firmly believe that young people should be taught to reserve sex for marriage, there is one area where I'm in agreement with the opponents of abstinence education: abstinence means nothing unless one understands exactly what it is. To that point, I would add that to understand what abstinence is, one must also understand what both sex and marriage really are—what they mean, and what they're for.

That all may sound simple enough, but growing up, I had no concept of the meaning and purpose of sex and marriage. I thought sex was something one did for recreation and also if one wanted to have a baby. Marriage, I believed, meant that one had a societal sanction to have sex with a particular person. Sex was better when one was in love, I imagined. Married people should have sex only with each other because—well, because it wasn't nice to cheat, plus cheating could lead to divorce, which I knew was a pain.

All those assumptions were based on what I witnessed in living with my mother and, to a lesser degree, in visiting my father. Both my parents believed in marital fidelity, and they believed that children deserved loving parents. At the same time, they had both been wounded by the failure of their own union, and their residual bitterness tainted the image of marriage that they passed on to me.

As a teenager with no moral foundation for my resolution to save my virginity for Mr. Right—other than a fear of being hurt by Mr. Wrong—I felt free to push the envelope. No, more than free; I felt *entitled* to push things, because I resented that God—if He existed—hadn't sent me my soul mate. I became a virgin who did "everything but."

When, at age twenty-three, I finally got tired of waiting and "officially" lost my virginity to a man I didn't love, it was a big deal to me at the time, but in retrospect it wasn't really so significant. True, my dalliances became less complicated. When I did "everything but," I used to dread having to explain why I didn't want to go all the way; once I started having sex, that was no longer necessary. But in a wider sense, losing my virginity, far from being the demarcation between past and future, was just a blip on the continuum of my sexual degradation. The decline had begun when I first sought pleasure for its own sake. It would continue until the day I became born again, at the age of thirty-one, and was jarred into consciousness of sin.

❧

Once, when I was about eight years old, I complained to my mother that I was sick of going over to see my dad on Saturday only to have him go out with my stepmother on my one night at his place.

I remember that Mom, in trying to figure out what to do, asked me what would be more painful—going to see Dad as I had been, with his going out at night, or not seeing Dad at all.

I had to think about that one before ultimately deciding it would be more painful not to see him.

Only a year later, the question would be moot. My father took a job across the country. From then on, I would see him only a week or two out of the year.

Even though I hadn't seen much of my father while he was in town, his move was heartbreaking for me. I remember one day in fourth grade, just before he moved, when I broke down crying in class. I knew that what little relationship I had with him was going to be severely impaired by the distance—and it was.

~⌘~

Two decades later, at age twenty-nine, when I was going through an especially blistering breakup, I had a realization so weighty that it felt like a major revelation. It hit me that I had brought the breakup upon myself by sabotaging the relationship.

My past experiences with men, I realized—both the one-night stands and the attempts at relationships—were based around the idea of choosing the lesser pain. My big fear was that boyfriends would leave me—just as I feared as a child that my father would lose interest in me if I failed to earn his affection.

Just as I knew that no matter how well I succeeded at earning Dad's affection, I'd have to go home when the weekend was out, so it was with love interests. However much I wanted a man to stay, I felt deep down that he was certain to leave.

The solution I unwittingly chose—I say unwittingly, because it was the opposite of what I consciously wanted—was to become an accomplice in my own rejection.

I told myself that if I was going to be hurt anyway, I might as well be able to see it coming. Seeking out men who were distant—whose affection I knew deep down I could never earn, though I desperately wanted to try—assured me of failure. I could then plunge into a brief, intense physical relationship, having all the excitement of a fulfilled crush—but knowing in my heart that it was too good to last.

My belief that my sexual relationships were doomed to self-destruct became a self-fulfilling prophecy. I felt so helpless that I would harm the relationship just so I could be in control. I would be careless, say and do things that were hurtful, embarrass myself, or get too intense too soon.

From my teens until I found my faith, I also suffered from clinical depression. That, together with my insecurity, created a feeling of desperation. Sometimes I would impulsively "act out." I was never violent, but I could be—ahem—a little obsessive. Somewhere, there is a man who remembers the day in 1996 when I showed up at his flea-market stall wearing a black curly Cher wig, black patent–vinyl biker cap, black patent–vinyl minidress, and coordinating black patent–vinyl thigh-high boots. It's all a blur to me now, but apparently, I was trying to win him back. (It didn't work.)

✎

At the same time that I began to realize how my parents' divorce had affected my actions and attitudes, something wonderful was happening in my life. My relationship with my father was healing.

My relationship with my mother had already undergone significant healing from when I was sixteen on. That was when she became a Christian and, wishing to live out her faith, began to practice chastity. She lived patiently that way for some time—it would be ten years before she would meet the man who became my stepfather. Although I couldn't identify with her chastity, I admired her faith and self-control, plus I was relieved that she was no longer risking being hurt by noncommittal men.

My father's change came about under the influence of my step-mother. This brave woman, whom I once resented for taking away my dad's attention, urged him to examine his relationship with my sister and me. He was surprised to learn that I did not feel particularly close to him—and that I'd always felt his love was based on conditions I could never meet.

The result was not a total transformation, but when your relationship's in darkness, a crack of light through the door can make all the difference. I felt for the first time that I could call my father and not have to just reel off my impressive achievements. At last, on a deeper level, he showed that he really cared about me and my life.

Although it would be three more years before I would accept the Lord and change my lifestyle, I have no doubt that my real journey to faith and chastity was jump-started by the healing of my relationship with my father. After he reconciled with me, it became much harder to convince myself that rejection was always a certainty. Cynicism was starting to get old.

〜✖〜

Whether your parents influenced you in a positive way, or whether you're trying to overcome your upbringing, your feelings about them will affect you as you work to change your life. Now, at the start of your journey, is a good time to examine what you've learned from them and what you need to unlearn. Here are a few things to think about as you consider where you came from and where you're going:

- **Instead of repeating your parents' mistakes, you can learn from them.** Knowledge is power. What negative messages did you receive as a child about your attractiveness, your intelligence, or the nature of sex and marriage? The more you understand how you were influenced by those messages, the more you will be able to view them from an older, wiser, and more objective perspective.

For example, my mother was extremely self-conscious about her weight when I was growing up. She passed her self-consciousness on to me, including her habit of weighing herself every morning. If you have that habit too, then you know that not only is it a very hard one to break, but it also carries a risk; a little gain gets your day off to a depressing start.

Every so often, a conscious decision *not* to weigh myself in the morning. I made the change just for the sake of breaking away from putting my daily self-image at the mercy of the bathroom scale. It's a freeing feeling, reminding me that my identity is more than whatever I may weigh at a given time. It also reminds me that as much as I may be influenced by my mother, I'm my own woman.

- **Someone was looking out for you—whether you wanted them to do so or not.** Chances are that at some point during your childhood, even if your parents were marauding hippies, Mom or Dad sat you down and tried to instruct you in chastity—or at least about what's right and wrong in relationships. What messages did you receive from your parents that ring true today? It may be that a parent tried to give you a moral message and you discounted it because you were annoyed at the messenger, or because you simply weren't interested. Doesn't it feel good now to realize that one of your parents cared enough about you to want to steer you on the right path? Now is as good a time as any to tell him or her thanks—and to say you're sorry you didn't listen before.

- **When all is said and done, your parents are human beings with human foibles.** One of the best spiritual gifts one receives in adulthood is the ability to see one's parents as people. My mother often asks me how I would feel to have children as old as my sister and I were when she was my age. I have to admit, I can't imagine. As I said before, it's only now that I'm beginning to understand what sex is for. The idea of having to explain it to kids is unfathomable. (It's hard enough explaining it to *adults*.) Gaining a wider perspective is essential if you're going to . . .

- **Forgive your parents.** Because they're not getting any younger, and neither are you. Also, because God says so. And, most important to where you are right now, because every effort you make to forgive your parents will bring you healing and strength for the journey ahead.

the meaning of sex

One day, when I was about eight years old, during a creative dramatics class where the teacher seemed willing to talk about anything, I blurted out a question that had been on my mind for a while:

"How did *sex* get started?"

The teacher, a woman in her twenties, was caught off guard. She hemmed and hawed for a moment, but I persisted:

"How did the first men and women figure out how to have sex?"

I still remember the teacher's attempt at an answer, because it was so odd. She made up something vague about how perhaps the woman gave off a certain smell that drew the man over to have sex with her. It sounded sufficiently gross to throw me off track, but it wasn't really an answer.

Eight years later, when I was a senior in high school, my question changed to the far more common "How do *I* start having sex?" But my experiences never taught me how sex got started—which is to say, *why* it got started. What is sex *for*?

We know that sex is for reproduction. A strict materialist—that is, someone who believes that all thoughts may be traced to physical causes—would tell you that the feelings of intimacy one has during sex are simply biological trickery to get us to want to propagate the species. (Why biology would care whether we propagate the species is never explained.)

On the other hand, if you believe that what transpires between a man and a woman during sex has its source in something other than the couple's DNA, their upbringing, and what they had for lunch, then sex must have a function that goes beyond creating more people to have sex.

During the past quarter century, Christianity has found a new way to state the answer to the question, what is sex for? It's called the "theology of the body." A deeply profound interpretation of basic principles found in the Bible, it's formulated in terms that contemporary people of faith can understand, and woven together like a seamless garment with the meaning of life itself.

First articulated by Pope John Paul II, the theology of the body is espoused by mainline Protestant denominations as well as Roman Catholicism. Focus on the Family, the Protestant ministry founded by Dr. James C. Dobson, offers several helpful articles based on the theology of the body at pureintimacy.org, and there are many good books on the subject, such as Christopher West's *Good News About Sex and Marriage*. These are fascinating, life-changing resources, and I can't recommend them highly enough if you're looking to explore what Christianity has to say about the deep and mystical meaning of sexual union between man and wife.

The theology of the body starts in Genesis, with God's creating man in His image. God is invisible. By giving us our bodies in His image, He has made the invisible visible, the intangible tangible.

So our bodies are living metaphors of God's loving nature—but more than metaphors, because God, in creating us, breathed His Spirit into us. This divine origin of our bodies gives what we do with them meaning beyond the superficial. When we use them as God has instructed us, especially when we take part in something sacred, we are making visible a hidden mystery—bringing to earth a bit of heaven. This may be seen in baptism, when, in being washed with water—the means we normally use to cleanse our bodies and make us feel new—we instead are cleansed in our souls and made into literally new creations. It may also be seen in Communion, when God uses the most mundane physical processes of eating and drinking to bring forth a metaphysical experience where we touch eternity.

To really see the theology of the body at work, you don't have to go inside a church. God uses your body every day to make the invisible visible and the intangible tangible. It happens every time you share His love with another individual.

I'm not talking about what Christians call witnessing. Ordinary acts of love and kindness—from telling a relative, "I love you," to smiling at the woman who sells you your morning coffee, to pausing to let another driver into your lane—all hint at heaven. Moreover, such actions align your body with God's purpose for it—a loving purpose that rejects selfishness.

The idea that parts of the body have purpose in and of themselves is not terribly fashionable these days. As our culture would have it, if a friend of yours gets her tongue pierced with a silver stud, you're not supposed to say, "That's gross. It looks unnatural, and it's going to be a real pain for you when you eat." You're supposed to say something like, "Cool! What a bold fashion statement!"

Likewise, our culture rebels against the idea that the body has a higher purpose, because to suggest it instantly implies that we will suffer in our spirits for sins that we commit against our own bodies.

This is too terrible for many people to even think about—so they deny the body's deeper meaning entirely.

Just as your tongue is made to taste and speak, so your whole body is made to experience God's love and communicate it to others. This is a great responsibility, but an even greater blessing—especially when we consider the most intense and exciting means that God has created for us to share His love.

In marriage, God enables us to use our bodies to create a love that is more than the sum of their parts. On one level, He does this literally—by granting children. But even before that occurs, He does it figuratively, by making the bride's and bridegroom's love bear new and greater spiritual fruit.

Jesus compared heaven to a wedding feast, and John wrote in the book of Revelation that we would all celebrate a wedding in heaven: the marriage of the church—which is to say, all believers who make it to heaven—to Jesus. When you unite yourself to a husband, you will in a very real sense be practicing for your life in heaven, united to the Lord in a way far beyond what you can imagine. Likewise, God intends your and your husband's love for each other to emulate His love for you—full, complete, and eternal.

One of the most beautiful and mysterious things about marriage is the fact that people get so excited about weddings even when they're not terribly religious. Why is that? I mean, when you go to a wedding reception, why are people so exhilarated if all they're celebrating is the fact that John and Judy can finally have socially sanctioned sex whenever they want? Why do people cry at weddings if they're only glad that Liz can have a kid before her biological clock runs out?

On some level, even if they don't fully understand it, people at weddings know that they are witnessing something greater than two people uttering timeworn phrases of fidelity. They know that even if John and Judy have been living together and already have a child, something changes once they're married. They're no longer mere individuals, but a couple, with the deepest, strongest commitment two people can have.

Now, if a couple who aren't even religious can feel somehow strengthened by the force of vows made before friends and family, imagine the force the marital commitment takes when made before the eyes of God. A man and woman's commitments to love, honor, and cherish each other as long as they both shall live take on new meaning and power when they both long with all their hearts for *eternal* life with God. The gift of self that they give to each other becomes a gift to the Lord.

God rewards the married couple with the gift of being able to participate in His act of creation. This is expressed in the gift of children, but also in the creative spirit that flourishes between the man and the woman. When a husband and a wife put their hearts, minds, spirits, and bodies together with no limits, the result brings a spiritual abundance that—used properly—makes the world a far richer place.

According to Orthodox rabbi Jay Spero of the Saranac Synagogue in Buffalo, New York, God uses the natural polarity between a married man and woman to right an unbalanced world. "When a man and a woman live together in harmony, and there is peace between them, the Divine presence dwells in their midst," Spero says. "The reason for this is that when you take two things which are by definition opposites and bring them together, this is a microcosm of the purpose of the creation of the world.

"We are put on this earth to bring it to a higher level, what is contemporarily called [in Hebrew] 'Tikkun Olam'—repairing the world," the rabbi continues. "When we take our body, which is something completely physical, and sanctify it with spirituality, we have taken two opposites and integrated them. This is done by performing [God's] commandments. And when this integration takes place between a husband and wife, there is no greater sanctification of the world."

With the belief that the body has a purpose, sex outside marriage truly becomes a blind alley. Christopher West, who has written several books on the theology of the body, describes it in an interview with the Web site Beliefnet.com as "telling lies with the body."

"I will be lying if I am having sex with someone to whom I am not married," West explains, "because my body is saying, 'I give myself to you freely, totally, faithfully and fruitfully'—that's wedding vows—but I haven't committed to that. I don't mean that in my heart. I'm saying something with my body that isn't true."

His comments remind me of a story my mother tells about an incident that happened when my sister was a toddler. Sis was playing with my mother on the sidewalk outside our house when a little boy who lived next door rode up on a tricycle and knocked her down.

My mother was horrified. As my sister sat crying, Mom looked up and saw the boy's mother looking out her window, smiling. Apparently the bully's mom thought it was all harmless fun.

Then the boy rode right up again—and hit my sister a second time.

My outraged mom knew she had to do something—but the bully's mother, her own neighbor, was still looking on.

So, Mom walked up to the boy with a saccharine smile on her face. With the smile glued in place, she gave the boy a big bear hug.

As her arms encircled him, Mom said, "Run over her again and I'll knock the [fecal matter] out of you."

That, my friend, is "lying with the body." Admittedly, it fulfilled

Mom's purpose; the boy never bothered my sister again. It worked because she intended it to be simultaneously deceptive and scary—and it was.

My mother's actions were more frightening than if she had merely yelled at the boy, because there's something deeply disturbing when one part of a person's body is saying something different from the rest of it. You've probably experienced it anytime you have been introduced to someone who smiled and said he or she was glad to meet you—but gave you a fishy handshake.

How much more disturbing, then, while you're engaging in the most intimate act with a man who is synchronizing his every breath and movement with your own, to know that—in a matter of minutes or hours—he'll say diffidently, "I'll call you."

One of the things about my father that touched my mother's heart was the way he would act when she was sad. Dad wasn't one to show great emotion. If something happened that made Mom cry, he would say to her, "Cry for me." He meant, "Show the emotion that I can't show." Unable to empathize, he could at least sympathize—by asking Mom to make her tears do double duty.

When you've been hurt by men, it's easy to generalize and say that they don't understand, they don't care, or they can't be hurt like you or I can. In a sense, that's true. But just as we can hurt in ways that men can't comprehend, they also feel pain in ways that are beyond our understanding. It's not just their egos that bruise easily. My father's reaction to my mother's tears taught me that men's inability to feel our pain can be painful for them.

As the old saying goes, women are soft on the outside and hard on the inside, while men are hard on the outside and soft on the inside.

It's no coincidence that a man—nineteenth-century opera composer Ruggiero Leoncavallo—created the timeless character of Pagliacci, the clown who laughs on the outside and cries on the inside. Some of the greatest male songwriters have made their careers with lyrics about the pain they hide, like Smokey Robinson with his classic Motown tunes "Tracks of My Tears" and "Tears of a Clown."

Now, I'm not going to tell you that behind every heartless womanizer lurks a wounded little boy. (As a friend of mine who's a crime journalist says, some people are just evil.) But you already know that you don't want a womanizer. You want the kind of man who's looking to find the right woman and settle down. With that as your desire, it's important to understand that however much men may seem able to detach emotion from sex, they *are* conscious of the emotional and spiritual power of the sex act. Ironically, that's why some men are womanizers—because they can't handle having sex with a woman they love.

For men, a key aspect of sex is the very thing women associate with it as well: vulnerability. It makes them feel exposed—not only literally but figuratively, as they're conscious of the possibility of ridicule and the pressure to perform.

Because of the way they are built and their ability to keep their emotions under wraps, men are able to have casual sex with fewer visible emotional repercussions than women. Yet, I believe the overall effect is ultimately much the same. They feel a hollowness, which they try to fill through fleeting sexual experiences. Because their dalliances never fill that hollowness, some men simply continue trying for new, same-but-different sexual experiences. The worst of them—womanizers and porn addicts—seem crippled and helpless, like drug-addicted lab monkeys who keep hitting a button for their next fix.

Thankfully, many single men are aware of the hollowness that casual sex holds—which is why they desire something better. Casual sex, they know, would leave them hungry, and they desire more than anything to be filled. For such a man, falling in love and marrying feels like finding his true home at last.

You may ask if such men really exist. I know they do, because I've met them; some are in my own family. Most of all, I know they exist because, for God's purpose for love and sex to be fulfilled, both men and women must be capable of experiencing both to the fullest.

saying yes like you mean it

Some people who don't really know what chastity means assume that it's too simplistic for sophisticated adults—a relic from the era when schoolkids were given the antidrug message "Just Say No." The truth is that it's far more nuanced. In the language of chastity, no means yes—and yes means no. I'm not talking about consent, but the issues behind consent. When you say yes or no, what are you really saying yes or no *to*?

Modern culture embraces relativism—the idea that my "truth" is no better than your "truth," and vice versa. But when it comes to sex, the tables are turned. So-called hipsters see things only in black and white—while the chaste counterculture sees boundless shades of gray.

You can see the contrast in perspectives through the way the popular culture equates chastity with abstinence. In reality, while abstaining from sex may be part of chastity, the chastity concept goes far beyond keeping one's thighs closed. It's a discipline that engages mind, body, and spirit.

One can be abstinent and not be chaste; I've been like that at times when I've let myself become preoccupied with sexual fantasies. Likewise, if one is married and treats one's partner with love, one can be chaste and not abstain from sex.

The relativists' idea of sex as being genital centered creates a neat dividing line, but it ultimately brings man down to the level of an animal whose sexual experience is limited to physical sensations. The chaste know that there is more to sex than slobber-slobber-huff-puff-push-push-bang. Likewise, they know that saying yes has far more layers of meaning than simply "Do me."

※

In his letter to the Philippians, Paul wrote, "Work out your own salvation" (2:12 NKJV). When I, at age thirty-one, first became aware of Christ's saving power, I had a *lot* to work out.

I knew that as a new Christian, certain things were expected of me. This gift of faith, which came unexpectedly, required me to strive upward. Although I had yet to understand the nature of chastity, I knew I had to stop allowing myself to use men or be used by them sexually.

And yet—there was a nagging voice inside my mind saying that sexual sins were pretty low on God's list of pet peeves.

I thought of the popular bumper sticker "Christians aren't perfect—just forgiven." In that light, I envisioned a sort of sexual safety net. Sounds kinky? It was. I decided I would really *try* to avoid premarital sex, but if I failed, I knew all I had to do was ask God for forgiveness. Then, by His own rules, He'd have to let me back onto heaven's waiting list.

What was lacking from my theology was an understanding of the nature of sin.

While my conversion had been dramatic—healing me not only

of my unbelief, but also of the depression that had plagued me since my teen years—I still had the wrong idea about what really happened when I broke a commandment. (Sex outside marriage breaks the commandment against adultery. If your heart's desire is that a man vow to love, honor, and cherish you for as long as you both shall live, then it breaks the golden rule as well.)

Without realizing it, I was treating God's rules as though they were arbitrary. Perhaps I thought they were there merely to protect me from possible earthly repercussions to bad behavior. In that light, God was a utilitarian, with the commandment against adultery merely a helpful hint to keep me from becoming jaded.

I first began noticing the holes in my sexual safety net about six months after becoming a Christian, while attending a crowded New York City music-collectors' fair. Over the noise of record and CD dealers and their customers, a familiar male voice with an English accent called out.

"Dawn!"

I turned and recognized an old flame I hadn't seen in a long time. "Jack" was an author in his forties, who chain-smoked Camels. Although I couldn't stand smoke, he had won me over with his wit, old-world charm, and good looks (he used to get mistaken for the French actor Gerard Depardieu).

I had been so taken with him that I'd gotten involved with him even after he told me he couldn't limit himself to only one woman. It was the worst mistake I'd ever made in a relationship—maybe my worst mistake, period.

Now, face-to-face with Jack for the first time in three years, I was consumed with shame.

Not wanting to show my feelings in public, I smiled and pretended nothing was wrong, telling him he looked great—he was thinner than I recalled. The look in his eyes told me I'd said the wrong thing.

Taking another look, I realized Jack wasn't just thin. His face was drawn, with deep lines that weren't there before.

He had a rare form of cancer—a variety, ironically, *not* connected to smoking.

Jack told me about how he was fighting the illness, changing his diet and so on. "I'm determined to beat this thing," he said. But there was something about the way he said it that made me realize he wouldn't.

Fingering my cross necklace nervously, I asked him if he was religious. He told me he wasn't in the least; in fact, he was very cynical about faith.

As a new Christian, I didn't know how to respond. Trying to remember the advice of the apostle Paul, I sputtered something about "mortifying the body" (see Romans 8:13). I meant that he should be chaste, but the way it came out, it sounded pretty morbid.

That was the last time I saw Jack. A year later, I read in a local paper that he'd died of his illness.

The thought of Jack unrepentant on his deathbed haunted me. For the first time, I started to wonder what effect my own actions when I was unchaste had on the men with whom I'd had sex. I might be forgiven—but what about them?

Even then, I had a very hard time getting the chastity message from my heart and mind to the rest of my body.

The turning point occurred two years ago, on a date with a fellow New York City journalist on whom I'd had a crush for some months.

I knew right off that Bill wasn't marriage material. He was a playboy, he didn't share my faith, and he was hung up on a woman he still called his fiancée even though she'd gotten cold feet and moved to Australia.

So, why was I with him at all? The answer's the classic excuse, one that, as a friend of mine puts it, would never hold up in court: "I was lonely, Your Honor." Once you allow yourself to be defined by your loneliness, it's a small step to violating your most deeply held beliefs.

Bill and I were on the couch in his West Village apartment, in the first stage of a process I knew well from my pre-Christian days. Our attraction, which had long simmered in public was finally, seemingly inevitably, bubbling to the surface.

He kissed me, and everything started happening pretty quickly. We were about a minute and a half away from moving to his bed when I suddenly broke free and stood up.

"I—I haven't done this in a while . . . and I'm feeling really uncomfortable," I said.

That probably would have been enough, but I had something inside that had to get out. Before I knew it, I was crying.

What had hit me was that by getting physical with Bill, I was dis-respecting God. The Lord had already chosen a man for me to marry, and I hadn't met him yet. To fool around with someone who was so clearly *not* the one God had chosen for me was to say to God, in effect, "You've been taking Your precious time. Well, I don't have to wait for You. In fact, I don't even think You're playing with a full deck. Since You're not giving me what I want, I'm going to take what I can get. So there, Mr. Omnipotent."

I explained all this to Bill, declaiming dramatically as I stood there on his living room carpet while he sat on his couch with a quizzical expression on his face. He must have been shocked, but he politely humored me as I composed myself and made my exit. I went home still lonely, but with a feeling that something had changed. For the first time, I realized that all the times I'd said yes, I'd really said no.

Each time I'd said yes to sex outside marriage, I had been also saying no to the friendship of God. More than that, I was denying my partner friendship with God, by enabling him to act in a way that went against God's will for him.

I say "friendship," because friendship is a two-way street. God is always ready to be our friend, but He can partner with us only if we allow Him to be Lord of every aspect of our lives. Jesus told His disciples, "If anyone loves Me, he will keep My word; and My Father will love him, and We will come to him and make Our home with him" (John 14:23 NKJV). The Holy Spirit can't make His home in you when you shut the door.

If you want to change your life for the better, you must be completely open to experiencing the blessings God has for you. That's why chastity isn't about saying no. It's about saying *yes*.

There have been many famous yeses over the years, from the laundry detergent, to "Yes, We Have No Bananas," *Yes, Virginia, There Is a Santa Claus,* and the Yes that recorded "Owner of a Lonely Heart." However, one yes in history towers above all others. You could say that it was the yes heard round the world.

The yes that changed everything was that spoken by Mary, when she told the angel Gabriel, "Behold the maidservant of the Lord! Let it be to me according to your word" (Luke 1:38 NKJV).

Gabriel had just told Mary that by the power of the Holy Spirit, her virgin womb would conceive the Son of God. Faced with this stunning announcement, the teenage girl had a choice. She could have disbelieved, she could have protested—she could have even said no.

Instead, Mary opened her heart to the Lord, putting herself at His service. Because she humbled herself to do God's will, He showered her with every blessing and grace.

What meaning does Mary's yes have for you and me? The answer is in that to which she said yes. She proclaimed her willingness to serve God right after the angel told her, "With God nothing will be impossible" (Luke 1:37 NKJV).

What's impossible for you right now? I'll tell you a few of the things that have seemed impossible for me:

- feeling confident
- feeling graceful
- feeling attractive
- feeling capable
- being patient
- having self-control
- meeting a man I want to marry
- sustaining a relationship
- getting married

None of these things comes naturally to me. I can't imagine accomplishing them all on my own strength.

I spent years grasping at straws, trying to become the kind of person I wanted to be and meet the man I wanted to meet by doing all the wrong things. How did I come to suspect they were the wrong things? Well, for one thing, they didn't work . . .

A well-known tongue-in-cheek definition of *insanity* is "doing the same thing over and over again and expecting a different result each time." That's why women's magazines, TV shows, and movies can all drive you crazy. They say all you have to do is change your hairstyle, hike up your skirt, learn a new "sex trick" (as if you were some kind of X-rated poodle), and then "he'll fall in love with you." And women fall for it. *I* fell for it. I went for years thinking that if only I were prettier, more graceful, more confident, more this or that, my future husband would fall in love with me.

No matter what I did, success was always out of reach. It was impossible.

As soon as I took Mary's yes as a model, a fundamental change swept over me.

On one level, my situation's the same as before: I'd still like to feel more attractive, graceful, and so on, and I still believe that the qualities I desire are impossible for me to achieve through my own efforts.

What's changed is not so much what I am, but what I am *becoming*.

For the first time in my life, I feel that I am growing to be more like the woman God wants me to be.

I used to try to change the things about myself that I didn't like, but I never really believed in my heart that I could change. It always seemed like an uphill battle. Now, when I long for confidence, patience, or any of the other things I desire, I truly believe that all of them are within my reach.

Saying yes to God's will for you means saying no to thoughts, words, and actions that separate you from Him. Yet, once you do say yes, all those other things become so much smaller and unimportant by comparison.

Picture yourself as a thirsty plant. By saying yes to God and to whatever He has in store for you, you are crying out for water. Once you receive it, you will for the first time bear the spiritual fruit you were meant to bear.

God has promised this "living water" to all who ask for it, and I have no doubt that includes you. After all, in the words of the apostle Paul, "All the promises of God in Him are Yes" (2 Corinthians 1:20 NKJV).

tender mercies:
reconnecting with your vulnerability

Saying yes to God is one challenge. Saying yes to a man is another.

By that, I mean finally letting a man under your skin—not in a pragmatic "Let's take things as they come and see how things work out" kind of way, but in a "This is it—I'm in love, and I'm in it for the long haul" kind of way.

You may think that, if anything, you fall in love too easily. It may appear to you that women who have premarital sex do so because they're more open to a relationship than those who embrace chastity.

I'm not going to deny that some single women are abstinent because they fear sexual intimacy. I call such women abstinent, not chaste, because there is no fear in chastity. However, when a single woman who wants to get married instead finds herself having dead-end sexual relationships, she's not trying to let men inside. She's trying to shut them *out*.

If you hunger for intimacy but fear rejection, it is much, *much* easier to let a man touch your body than to let him touch your heart.

Village Voice sex columnist Rachel Kramer Bussel has admitted as much. "I will offer my body much sooner than my heart," she once wrote in her Lusty Lady column, "because I can walk away from casual sex, no matter how strong the connection, and not find myself crying, waiting for the phone to ring, or contemplating the other person's mindset."

Such rationalizations are all too familiar among single women, because they create an enticing fantasy: all you have to do is lower your expectations and you, too, can enjoy all the passion and excitement of casual sex, feeling no pain from the inevitable separation.

I tried very hard to buy into that fantasy, because I believed that a man was more likely to fall in love with me after having sex than prior to it. More than that, I had a sense of entitlement. I *deserved* a soul mate. If God wasn't keeping up His end of the bargain by sending me one, then I believed I had every right to take my pleasure where I could get it.

My mentality was akin to that of a little girl who's been good for a whole day and believes that she deserves ice cream. So Mom and Dad won't take me to Baskin-Robbins? I'll show them! I'll pig out on Marshmallow Fluff.

I admit it's possible to achieve the fantasy of casual sex with no apparent emotional consequences—just as it's possible to eat Marshmallow Fluff for three meals a day and never get cavities. In the case of the sugary foodstuff, you won't get any cavities if you eat while wearing a boxer's mouth guard. Likewise, with casual sex, you won't get hurt—as long as you adopt a hard shell. But if you do that, you're opening yourself up to a painful irony.

I discovered the irony myself, late in the game: the same armor that enabled me to tolerate casual sex made me less attractive to the kind of man I most desired.

Men with depth quickly figured out that I took sex far too lightly. Worse, I became so used to viewing myself and potential partners as objects of physical desire that I became unable to give of myself. Against my heart's own wishes, I tried to drag new relationships down to the lowest common denominator—and then wondered why the most sensitive and feeling men wouldn't stay with me.

To this day, when I see a woman at a party break into drunken kisses with a handsome man she's just met—or even take him home—part of me envies her. It's a druglike thrill to suddenly break down the physical barriers with a man. Even since becoming chaste, there have been countless times when, while talking with a cutie, I've thought about how easy it would be to suddenly shock him with a boundary-smashing smooch.

When tempted in that way, thinking back to the days when I was having casual sex puts me back on terra firma. During those days, I still slept alone more often than not. When I did, the nights were lonelier than they are now, because after every pseudo-relationship, I was back to square one. No matter how much of an expert I became at the art of hooking up (and let me tell you, despite what *Cosmo* may claim, it doesn't take any high-level skills), I wasn't getting any better at having a real relationship—and I knew it.

The realization that I had blunted my emotions for the sake of physical pleasure helped me gain the strength to resist casual sex.

Healing the damage takes time—but there are some fun surprises along the way. The biggest surprise for me has been discovering how much there is to *like* about men.

I now notice things about the men in my life that I never noticed before, like their thoughtfulness, their love of family, their integrity, even their vulnerability. These are intangible qualities that don't jump out at you when you're in a frame of mind where you're viewing men only as potential dates. Put together, they add up to character. It's the most important quality to seek in a husband, and the one that's least discussed in this day and age.

Likewise, when you become chaste, you'll notice for the first time that women who have sex outside marriage don't really appreciate men. You can't see this when you're having premarital sex, because you don't realize how much there really is about men to appreciate. You think that the mere fact that you're attracted to them and they seem to wield such power over you shows you appreciate them for what they really are. From there, it's a short step to the cynical stereotype we all know from popular culture—the worldly-wise, "been there, done that" single woman who doesn't trust men any farther than she can throw them.

On television and in movies, if a single woman is friends with a man, the pal is more often than not a homosexual. The message is that heterosexual men aren't capable of friendship, or even worthy of it. In contrast, gay men are depicted as safe and nonthreatening, trustworthy, and having more to give than straight men.

Imagine if the tables were turned. Imagine watching a TV sitcom where all the gay men are Neanderthal lunkheads, while the kind, thoughtful straight men are always ready to help their female friends without asking sexual favors in return.

If you saw a show like that, you'd think the producers really had it out for gay men. Yet many women tolerate such stereotyping against straight men, because they're conditioned to expect "manly men" to lack character. Part of this conditioning comes from the media, but a large part of it—I'd say, most—comes from such women's own warped perspectives, brought about by the superficial nature of their dating experiences.

When I had premarital sex, I became accustomed to seeing myself as a commodity—a varied collection of looks, wit, intellect, and *je ne sais quoi*. I looked for men whose commodities were worth as much as my own.

Most of all, I looked for men whose commodities were readily apparent. The singles scene isn't known for its subtlety. Men who were reserved or modest, who didn't flirt readily, who weren't attuned to my single-gal vibe—the nature of my casual-sex mind-set forced them all out of the running.

Is it any surprise, then, that I tended to date narcissists? And that I believed if I let them reach me emotionally, they would hurt me? So, I built up walls of protection. I thought I was "guarding my heart."

Today, I see those walls for what they really are—and they look like poorly installed weather insulation. They don't do anything they're supposed to do. The chill winds of rejection seep through, while the warm breezes of love are muffled.

I still have a lot to learn about sustaining a lasting relationship, but I firmly believe that during the time I've spent working at chastity, the hardness that men perceived in me has been gradually melting away. In its place are an openness and a vulnerability that make me more susceptible to being hurt, yet infinitely more capable of sustaining more than just a relationship, but a *vocation*—the vocation of marriage.

∽∞∾

When I was thirteen, my mother and I visited London, where we took a day trip in a boat on the Thames. Every so often, the boat would have to stop at a lock. I remember the locks as being sort of like little dams. They had doors that would gradually admit water into the section of the river where we were, until the boat was level enough to glide through it to the next section.

I think of being in love as like being on that Thames boat, urged along by the current, until I hit one of the locks. Then I have to wait for the water to pour in, taking me up and through to the next level. Ultimately, I keep getting farther along, and the water keeps getting deeper. But I have to get through the locks, one at a time.

Fears, like locks, can leave one feeling dead in the water. But, as the self-help slogan goes, feelings aren't facts. My mother puts it a better way: they're not the truth. The truth is always love, and love, contrary to popular belief, is not a feeling. Love is a *presence*.

Think about how we get the sun's light. From our perspective, the sun's light bends according to the hours and the seasons. Within the course of a single day, the shadow on a sundial will turn full circle.

Doing a "360"—that's what we humans call passionate. The sun's changes may be predictable, but they're radical all the same.

Yet, the sun never moves. It's only because *we* move that its shadows appear to be so capricious.

It's the same with God. He's the same yesterday, today, and forever. But how we position ourselves in relation to Him can change our whole lives.

Are you in a position today where, like a plant on a windowsill at high noon, you're able to receive God's direct sunlight? Or are you approaching God at an angle, letting His light hit you in some places while jealously guarding the rest of yourself in shadow?

Don't be shy. I have my shadows—lots of them. Every time I begrudge someone for making me move my bag from the subway seat next to me so he can sit down, that resentment is a shadow. Every time I congratulate myself on my self-control while being jealous of those who enjoy pleasures that I've forsaken, that's a shadow (two, actually—pride and envy). Every time I say or e-mail something dismissive to someone for no reason other than that she bugs me, that's a shadow. And every time I resent someone for not being something he couldn't possibly be if he tried, that's a shadow.

It's hard to release our shadows, partly because we're comfortable the way we are—maybe not happy, but comfortable. More than that, we may not trust that God *could* enlighten our darkness if we asked Him—and the thought of being disappointed by Him deters us from taking the chance.

Someone like me, who believes in God yet holds on to some shadows, is acting on the assumption that God has the power to change some areas of our lives, but not others. While it's true that we can't rely on the Lord to answer every specific need in our lives, there are certain spiritual blessings of His that are *always* available from God through the Holy Spirit. What's more, He dispenses them more readily—and liberally—than we can imagine. Here are just four of them:

- **Wisdom.** "For the LORD giveth wisdom: out of his mouth cometh knowledge and understanding" (Proverbs 2:6 KJV). "If any of you lack wisdom, let him ask of God, that giveth to all men liberally, and upbraideth not; and it shall be given him" (James 1:5 KJV).

- **Strength.** "I pray that out of his glorious riches he may strengthen you with power through his Spirit in your inner being" (Ephesians 3:16 NIV).

- **Hope.** "May the God of hope fill you with all joy and peace as you trust in him, so that you may overflow with hope by the power of the Holy Spirit" (Romans 15:13 NIV).

- **Endurance.** "May the God who gives endurance and encouragement give you a spirit of unity among yourselves as you follow Christ Jesus" (Romans 15:5 NIV).

Yet, even those blessings, which I request in prayer every day, aren't really necessary if I take God's little shortcut: recognizing and becoming part of the presence that is His love. I call it "God's little shortcut" because no other gift He gives is complete without it, and by itself it surpasses all gifts.

The idea of love as a presence and not a passion is tantalizingly similar to the definition of faith given to us in Hebrews: "the substance of things hoped for, the evidence of things not seen" (11:1 NKJV). It gives love a tangibility and a certainty that we normally do not feel in everyday life, save for the moments when we contemplate those dearest to us. More than that, love as a presence suggests something that's inescapable, without form—something that could conceivably fill everything.

The thought of this flowing presence is a comfort when I confront my own fears and insecurities—the Thames-like locks that prevent me from giving of myself. It helps immeasurably to know that while the locks may discourage me, the river of love exists whether I feel it or not. Most important, the locks don't go on forever. I know with all my heart that on this very river I'm on, one day I will pass through one of them and discover that it opens up into the sea.

the iniquity of my heels: a sole in danger

Blogger Charles G. Hill of Dustbury.com observes that whether you believe the influence of *Sex and the City* was positive or negative, it can't be denied that "the former HBO series did have some impact on popular culture, to the extent that it's had some small but measurable effect on women's shoes, pushing them a notch or two in the direction of sheer frivolity."

I was reminded of that aspect of the show's influence on my way home from my late-night newspaper job, traversing the dark streets in my Easy Spirit Level 2 walking shoes. (Level 2 is for "advanced walkers with medium-intensity activities.") I was reading Psalm 49, where I found the kind of deliciously mysterious question typical of King David's verse: "Wherefore should I fear in the days of evil, when the iniquity of my heels shall compass me about?" (v. 5 KJV).

"The iniquity of my heels." I know exactly what that means. It's a personal message for me. We'll get to that.

But dang if it isn't a *perfect* metaphor for those *Sex and the City* gals too.

The show's character Carrie, played by Sarah Jessica Parker, literally "Carries" the weight of singlehood—on the balls of her feet. She's notorious for wearing ultraexpensive designer shoes with heels the diameter and length of ballpoint pens. The shoes cram her toes into a tiny point—something that Parker apparently could withstand naturally, but it proved so difficult for her imitators that podiatrists began to offer toe-sawing surgery.

❧

As any high-heel aficionado could tell you, the shoes' cachet goes well beyond their designer brand. High heels alter a woman's posture, making her appear more vulnerable in every way—from the obvious way they make her teeter, bounce, and take shorter steps, to the subtler ways they cause parts of her to draw in and others to stick out.

As a result, for the woman who would be Carrie, the "iniquity of her heels" really does catch up with her. The shoes that the TV icon favors—again, not ordinary pumps, but mile-high teetering spikes—present the wearer as a helpless, submissive would-be sex partner—hence the unprintable street nickname given to them. (If you must know, they're "—— me pumps.") From there, they almost inevitably end up directing the wearer's behavior. She clearly positions herself as an object—and so she treats others like objects as well. Once you present yourself as a means to an end, you're forced to view others through that same superficial lens.

So where does that leave me in my clunky, old-lady Easy Spirits? Actually, not so far from Carrie—only on the other side of the same razor-thin Manolo Blahnik spike.

The jaded bed-hoppers' escapades on *Sex and the City* may be fictional, but the show's popularity is largely because single women can identify with the protagonists' shared pathology. The characters' sense of being separate from one another and from God—part of the human condition—is amplified in their dark and insidious fear of rejection.

That point was driven home to me recently when I was jolted awake from a disturbing dream in the middle of the night. I realized I'd had this same dream many times before, only it had escaped my waking memory.

It was a dream of holding a man very tightly as he lay on top of me in bed. We weren't having sex, just tied in an embrace. He was formed like a majestic Renaissance sculpture—Michelangelo's *David* come to life. I could see his ivory, almost translucent skin and his back. His chin was over my left shoulder, so I couldn't see his face. The feeling of his back and shoulder under my right hand was wonderful, and utterly real.

But then my waking mind began to return and I realized I hadn't gone to bed with anyone. I knew I was in a dream state, and I started to fear that I was actually being molested by an intruder. So I began to awaken myself, opening my eyes . . .

. . . and the dream-man started to melt away.

Immediately, I felt this terrible sensation of loss, and I tried to stop myself from waking. But it was too late—I was alone in bed, the sensation of a man's presence gone.

The only thing that stayed with me was that last, awful sensation of feeling the flesh under my hand evaporate—and the helplessness of not being able to stop it. I wanted so badly to hold on to this phantasm, but I couldn't.

Only later, as I pulled out my pocket Gideons Bible to look at Psalm 49 while padding down the dark streets, did the meaning hit me: the iniquity of *my* heels is a fear of rejection—embodied in that pathetic grasping at air.

∾⟳∾

Since I was only five at the time, I don't remember the day my father moved out of the house. Practically speaking, it may not have made much difference to me—his job took him out of town much of the time anyway. But I do remember what it was like for my sister and me to grow up with a single mother who carried the scar left by her failed marriage.

And so, my reality from age five to my mid-twenties was that my parents' divorce had left my mother lonely and—despite her best efforts—unable to meet a man who would commit, while my father was emotionally distant.

Over time, both parents' situations would change; Mom would wed a man who committed himself fully to her, and Dad would make a deep and sincere effort to reach out to me. But the child is mother to the woman, and the circumstances in which we grow up determine how we react to the world. I grew up believing that marriages don't last, men come and go as they please, and the most desirable men are the least attainable.

∾⟳∾

Even as a teenager beginning to date for the first time, I wasn't stupid. I knew that I had preconceptions about men that went against my fantasy of falling in love and getting married. To tell the truth, I knew I had a pathological fear of rejection practically before I was ever rejected. It was what I didn't know that would really hurt me.

What I didn't begin to realize until my late twenties—after enduring about as many breakups as Carrie and her pals go through in the first two seasons of *Sex and the City*—was that there's a flip side to the fear of rejection. It's the fear of intimacy.

Before I discovered that flip side, if you'd asked whether I feared intimacy, I would have immediately gone on the defensive. How could I be afraid of intimacy, when it was nearly always me who got dumped?

If anything, I thought, my problem was not that I was distant myself, but that I chose distant men. Often they were *literally* distant. Working in the music business, I had a knack for meeting musicians or music journalists who lived across the country or even across the ocean.

That was the little recording that reverberated in my head all the years I played the dating game: intimacy isn't my problem; it's *theirs*.

Then, when I was twenty-nine and going through yet another painful breakup with yet another long-distance boyfriend, something broke me out of my vicious circle.

⤫

Every so often, if you listen to your conscience, it will tell you something that you've really known all along, but were unwilling to admit to yourself.

I listened to my conscience one day, and it told me why nearly all my relationships had been so brief—and why I'd had so many one-night stands.

It said that I had a fear of intimacy. The fear, I realized, stemmed from the knowledge that if I let a man get under my skin, I would become vulnerable to the crushing blow of rejection.

In that light, my one-night stands, which had seemed so spontaneous and passionate, suddenly became cold and clinical. They weren't about excitement, but about control.

I longed for closeness, but couldn't take the risk. If a breakup was inevitable—and I was convinced in my heart that it was—then the best way to protect myself was to speed up the entire relationship.

Since a man wouldn't take me seriously if I slept with him too soon, I'd sleep with him right away. That way, when I left his apartment in the morning I would know that there was no need to leave any things of mine behind. There'd be no uncertainty. The pain of separation would come, but it wouldn't hit me so deeply, because I'd see it coming.

That realization was the beginning of my healing. No longer could I put the blame on others for my loneliness. Instead, in the words of *Pogo* cartoonist Walt Kelly, "We have met the enemy and he is us."

There's yet another dimension to the fear of rejection, and it can hit you even if you're the one doing the rejecting. It's the fear of letting go.

I remember when, as a preteen, I found a copy of J. D. Salinger's *The Catcher in the Rye* on my mother's bookshelf and read it for the first time. Even at that young age, I was struck by the book's ending, where Holden Caulfield warns that if you ever recount your experiences to someone, you'll start missing everybody.

Something about Salinger's words haunted me. In a way, it still haunts me today, even as I pray for God to bring my longings in line with His will.

It's because I've always had a fear of losing people—not only my loved ones, but anyone who's ever meant something to me, even if I'm no longer close to that person.

One way that I've tried to hold on to past relationships is by saving letters from former boyfriends. It didn't matter whether I was the one who initiated the breakup or not—every mushy note, every cheesy birthday card, every casual e-mail was preserved.

A few years ago—about the same time that I began to confront my fear of intimacy—I began to realize that by saving those letters, I was reinforcing my own insecurity. It was as though I felt I needed proof that someone, somewhere, had once cared about me. By holding on to such trophies, I was holding on to the fear that no man would ever care about me again. So, little by little, I started to destroy those old notes, cards, and e-mails whenever I would find them.

To actually destroy a letter from a former boyfriend felt terrible. I would sometimes cry as I did it. It was like the boyfriend's feelings for me were somehow still alive until I killed them by tearing up his letter—or, if it was an e-mail, hitting Delete.

But once the dirty deed was done, you know what? Relief.

It was as if a weight had been taken off my shoulders. I could finally let go.

∾

Letting go of a real live ex-boyfriend is another matter.

I broke up with my last boyfriend after dating for six months. It was yet another long-distance relationship, and as a result, it took me a long time to recognize personality differences that would have emerged quickly had he lived nearby. Even though I knew it was the right decision, I had to stop myself nearly every day from writing or calling him. I wish I could say it was because I missed him . . . but it wasn't.

The reason I wanted to reach him was because I wanted to know that he still cared about me in some way.

I couldn't stand the thought that a man who once lit up at the sound of my name, who took an avid interest in the most minute details of my daily life, could gradually lose concern for me.

There was also the possibility that he might be mad at me for initiating the split, but the thought of that didn't worry me the same way. It wasn't anger I was afraid of. It was apathy.

At times like that, I feel an emptiness inside myself—and I realize that if I follow my temptation to hold on to the man who's departed from my life, that emptiness will never be filled.

The truth is, I am not entitled to have a man care about me. The fact that I do believe the right one *will* care about me and will be my husband is not because I deserve it, but because enduring love between a man and a woman redounds to God's glory.

There's no sin in wanting to be loved. Iniquity comes from allowing our desire to rule over us, to the point that we separate ourselves from God, pursuing something or someone other than His best for us. My fear of letting go, then, is iniquity, because it makes me long for a man I can't marry, or one whom I know in my heart I shouldn't marry.

The apostle Paul compares a life in faith to a race: "Do you not know that those who run in a race all run, but one receives the prize? Run in such a way that you may obtain it" (1 Corinthians 9:24 NKJV).

That's why it's so important to address the iniquity of your heels—any emotional insecurity that's dogging you—*before* you attempt to begin a new relationship. Trying to go the distance when you're beset by fears makes as much sense as trying to run a marathon in four-inch stilettos.

∽∾

One wonderful thing about being in a growing relationship is that turning point where you realize the other person is not going away. Or at least that he doesn't intend to go away, and you don't intend to, and therefore you can lower the alert level of your fear of rejection from code red to orange, or even yellow.

The longer you're out of a relationship, the easier it becomes to forget that your ability to enter a relationship is dependent on your ability to get over your fear. It sounds like a paradox, and to some extent it is; being attracted to someone includes in its nature the desire not to be separated from that person. Yet, it's possible to cultivate a fear of rejection to the point where it becomes effectively another person in the relationship. And like the imaginary lover in my dream, the more you hold on to it, the lonelier you become.

Oh, yes, my imaginary lover. After I awoke in the middle of the night and realized that I'd had the same dream many times—and that it always ended in my waking up lonely, grasping at thin air—I determined never to have it again.

The next time I had that dream about the sexy mystery man who would always pull a last-minute disappearing act, I actually ordered him away before he could disappear.

The experience left me with a sense of victory—like the time when, in the midst of my umpteenth nightmare about being forced to redo high school, I suddenly exclaimed, "Wait a minute, this is crazy! I'm not in high school anymore! I've graduated!"

In the same way that I never had another high-school nightmare, so my Mr. Disappearing Act hasn't come back. I don't miss him.

Sometimes I try to act as if I've gotten over my fear of rejection, but it seems as though the wiser I pretend to be, the more the iniquity of my heels encompasses me. When it comes down to it, once you become dissatisfied with your own behavior, only two things will give you the wisdom and motivation to make necessary changes: time and prayer.

After the mention of "heels," Psalm 49 goes on to say, "God will redeem my soul from the power of the grave" (v. 15 NKJV). I take that and other promises to mean that He begins His redemptive work on me while I'm on *this* side of the grave—molding me into His likeness and transforming my weakness into strength.

God also says to pray always and to not lose heart (see Luke 18:1). Perhaps that's His way of keeping me on my toes.

eleven
up close and personal

The other night, I ran into a woman I know who informed me she was so dissatisfied with the caliber of men she was meeting through her social circle that she had joined a personal-ad Web site.

Unfortunately, she added, the site—one of the biggest in the business—had so far turned out to be a bust. The five responses she'd received in her ad's debut week ranged from the perverted to the inane. But what could she expect? According to a survey on the site, she was compatible with only 4 percent of its members.

Just a lonely little 4 percent. How sad. I gave her the requisite "poor baby" platitudes.

It wasn't until I got home that it hit me.

Assuming that the Web site's statistics hold true for real life, and assuming that what I learned in fifth-grade math still holds, Personal Ad Gal can theoretically walk into any room containing twenty-five men and discover one case of mutual boat-floating.

It boggles the mind.

Certainly, 4 percent is a far higher number of potential Mr. Rights than I want or need. In fact, I can't imagine being happy in a world where the odds of a man being my life mate were *greater* than one in one *billion*.

Think about it. What does it mean to believe that there is more than one man in the world whom you could marry?

Granted, you *could* marry any single man. There are probably several men you know who would give serious thought to the prospect if you popped the question right now—and that's not even counting the teenager who compliments your smile as he sells you your afternoon latte.

Believing that there is more than one man you could marry in God's eyes, however, is a different idea entirely. The idea presumes that God is merely a detached presence who looks on benignly as you muddle through life.

Au contraire. I believe that God is a matchmaker—and I believe His dossier on your possible candidates for a future husband is extremely thin. In fact, I believe it contains only one name.

∽∞∾

The idea of bride and groom being predestined for each other is not, as some would tell you, a creation of medieval romantic literature, nor is it a fantasy of the Victorian era. It dates back at least eighteen hundred years, to when the Jewish sage Rabbi Phineas wrote, "We find in the Torah, in the Prophets, and in the Holy Writings, evidence that a man's wife is chosen for him by the Holy One, blessed be He."[10] For proof, he pointed to Scriptures such as Proverbs 19:14: "Houses and wealth are inherited from parents, but a prudent wife is from the LORD" (NIV).

I imagine it this way: God is preparing a beautiful, romantic candlelight dinner for my future husband and me. It is taking Him an awfully long time to do this because everything has to be arranged just as He wants it. I can see the table, perfectly set with the finest china and tall, burning candlesticks—but I can't yet see the man who will join me there.

For me to then act out of desperation, chasing after available men—it's like grabbing the corners of the tablecloth, upsetting the gorgeous china setting for two, and putting out a Tupperware buffet instead.

In the film *Big Fish*, a boy sees a vision of his own death. That knowledge gives him supernatural confidence throughout life. In his moments of greatest fear, he can reassure himself by remembering, "This is not how I go."

Single women are told to view single men with an open mind, as though each one might be the One. I submit that this is counterproductive. When the difference between the right man and the almost-right man is analogous to the difference between lightning and a lightning bug, and when one faces the daunting task of weeding out 999,999,999 almost-right ones, the answer is not to keep playing the field.

Until lightning strikes, the answer is to keep remembering: "This is not how I go."

What goes through your head when you enter a room at a social event where you have the opportunity to meet a number of new men?

If you're like I used to be, you cast your gaze from man to man, thinking, That *one's handsome* . . . That *one's with someone* . . . That *one's too old* . . . That *one's got a scraggly beard—yuck* . . . That *one's got a wedding ring* . . . That *one looks too interested in the man he's speaking to* . . . and so on.

Without even thinking, I would run through the possibilities, narrowing down the field to the ones who seemed most attractive and most approachable. Then, depending on how gutsy I felt, I would either strike up a conversation with one of the possibilities, or try to get a friend to introduce me, or hang around him and hope he'd talk to me.

And so it went, until every possibility proved impossible—or until one of them thought I was a possibility as well. That's dating, meat-market style, and it's how we've been trained to believe romances get started.

Now, try to imagine what would happen if you walked into that same room convinced that, in all likelihood, you *weren't* going to find a love interest—let alone the love of your life. Suppose your only plan was to enjoy friendly conversation from men and women alike. How would you act differently?

You'd still find yourself drawn to men you considered attractive—it's only natural. But you'd be free from the pressure of having to find a way to speak with them. You'd also be liberated from the fear of disappointment if the evening produced no romantic prospects.

For me, putting this approach into action began like a parlor game: I would enter the room and try to see how long I could go before I placed myself strategically close to a man I wanted to meet.

When I'd find myself attracted to a man who was across the room, instead of drifting within his range, I would chat with the other men and women around me. Before I knew it, I was enjoying the conversation.

What usually happens at the point where I'm having a good time without pursuing anyone is that the man I want to meet will approach *me*—or, at least, he'll join in my conversation.

But what if you're strongly drawn to a certain man in the room and he *doesn't* come your way?

In your mind, you might reel off the possible reasons why: He may be shy, preferring the woman to make the first move. He may even think you're out of his league. Or he may simply not be interested. But before you decide to take your chances and introduce yourself to this handsome stranger, stop and think.

You've been within twenty-five feet of him for half an hour or more, and he's passed up every opportunity to meet you. Suppose he *is* shy—do you want a man who lacks initiative? Really, how hard is it for a man to smile at a woman and say hello?

Another thing to keep in mind if the man who has caught your eye fails to make a move is that he may very well already be in a relationship. If he is, he knows that being passive gives him plausible deniability. It's part of the unwritten Guy Rules. If you approach him, he can allow you to pick him up. Then, if his girlfriend or wife finds out, he can say he was seduced. It's an all-too-common game and, for you, a surefire way to get hurt.

But if you must approach a stranger, remember that table set for two. He might be the man for whom the table's set, or he might not. No matter what transpires between you and him, the setting is still awaiting only two guests at the appointed time. Keep that in mind and you can enjoy the excitement of meeting someone new, while resisting the temptation to tug at the tablecloth's corners.

❦

Where some women feel freedom in the realization that they ultimately have no control over where and when they'll meet their future husbands, others feel only fear. They are the ones who bankroll the singles industry as they answer personal ads, seek men online, and line up at speed-dating events. I was one of them myself—until I got wise.

Think about it. Since the start of the sexual revolution in the 1960s, the singles industry has flourished. Personal ads run in practically every newspaper from the *New York Times* on down, matchmaking services routinely send out "Dear Occupant" solicitations, and even the smallest of small-town community centers host speed-dating nights. With such a wealth of opportunities to meet one's soul mate, women must be marrying at a young, fertile age, and staying married. Right?

If you believe that, I've got an expired Match.com membership to sell you. Today's late-marrying women give the fertility clinics a booming business, and the divorce rate has skyrocketed. That's because the consumer tools that our culture claims empower single women actually *keep* them single—by encouraging women and men to view one another as commodities rather than human beings.

When you go on a date with a man you met through the singles industry—that is, a personal ad, matchmaking service, or singles event, a little voice in the back of your head says to your date, "*You can be replaced.*" Your date hears this voice even when you don't verbalize it—and you know he's got a voice in the back of his head as well, saying the same thing about you.

Even worse are speed-dating events. Talk about commoditizing human beings! The very nature of speed dating transmogrifies you from a unique child of God to a leg of lamb on a conveyor belt.

When you rely on the singles industry for your dates, placing yourself in the situation of constantly evaluating and being evaluated, it's so easy to become jaded. A layer of trust is removed, because both you and your date know just how easy it is for each of you to move on to your next "match."

There are exceptions. I know a woman who met her husband through the Jewish personals Web site JDate.com, and another who met hers through CatholicMatch.com. But when your goal is lifelong marriage, such extraordinary means should be used only as a last resort. The personals pond has too many frogs and not enough princes, plus—with its membership fees—it could leave you soaked.

If you do consider using a matchmaking service or personal ads, there are three important factors that must be present for your protection. The service should do the following:

- It should be affiliated with your faith. I don't just mean it should have an option so Christian applicants may choose to meet only Christians, or so on. The service must be *expressly* for people of your faith, and no one else. That requirement increases the likelihood that the men who apply will be serious about their faith as well as serious in their desire to get married.

- It should screen applicants personally. This rules out Web sites that allow anyone to post his or her information without any outside approval. There must be a point in the application process at which a real person sees the information that clients submit and judges whether or not he or she may sign up with the service.

- It should be exclusively for heterosexuals wishing to get married. This rules out all services that give clients the option of seeking casual dates, "activity pals," "swingers," and the like.

Violate these rules at your own peril. The singles bars are filled with bitter men and women in their forties who lost their hopeful spark from too many casual dates with strangers they met through the singles industry.

This attitude—that meeting your husband requires you to refrain from trying too hard—is not fatalistic. No one's asking you to hole yourself up in a castle, like Sleeping Beauty. What you can and should do, every day, is be yourself—not in the touchy-feely, Oprah sense, but in the sense of being who you are in God.

You were created with a unique personality—and the capacity to express it creatively. By that, I don't mean just through creative endeavors, but through every word you say and everything you do. Most of all, you are able to let your light shine before men and women. It's really God's light, but He enables you to shine it through the filter of your own individual character.

You want a husband who will be drawn to the light that is in you.

If your light shines through everything you do, from the greatest thing to the smallest, then it will be impossible for anyone to miss it. This is why the self-advertisement encouraged by the singles industry is counterproductive. When you focus the spotlight on yourself, no one can see how beautifully your light illuminates those around you.

It took me years to learn that lesson.

On a perfect May evening in 1992, as the sunlight began to dim, I stood outside the Sun Mountain Café on West Third Street, a twenty-three-year-old rock historian strumming a guitar that was older than me. I was getting ready to sing and play at the club's open mike, as I did every Tuesday—not because I thought I had a future as a performer, but because it was a fun way to meet guys.

This was during the time of my life when I was terribly depressed and lonely. Having given up on finding someone to love me in the foreseeable future, I worked instead to perfect what I saw as the art of having casual sex without getting hurt. (I never succeeded in getting that numb and detached, thank God—but even trying messed me up for years.)

"Hey, Dawn!"

I looked up from my guitar to see Richard—a cute musician I'd known casually for five years. No, not *that* way—we'd never so much as kissed.

Back when I'd first met Richard, I did pursue him, but his behavior made it clear early on that he liked me only as a friend. It was okay—I'd gotten that reaction from other men, and usually managed to stay friendly with them. By the time he spotted me that evening outside Sun Mountain, my attraction to Richard had long dissipated.

I told him that I was about to go onstage, but if he wanted to see me perform, then he could join my friend Babs, who was already inside.

It was natural for Babs to offer to come down to see me play. She was (and is) that kind of friend—a real cheerleader, always there for the people close to her.

Babs was five years older than I was; with her gentle, reassuring manner, she felt in many ways like an older sister. She was pretty, not in an artificial, model kind of way, but in a natural and sweet way. Her modesty—as well as her superthick Queens accent—belied the fact that she was as smart as a whip, with a wickedly funny sense of humor.

For all she had going for her, and despite her wanting to be married, there was no special man in Babs's life. Indeed, during the four years that we'd been friends, she'd hardly seen anyone beyond an initial dinner date—despite attempts by me and other friends to introduce her to men. It wasn't that she was too picky—she just wanted love and wasn't willing to settle for anything less.

I thought at the time that Babs wasn't trying hard enough. Twenty-eight seemed like a terribly advanced age to not be married. Instead of going out and trying to pick up a man, she was busy doing things like being a good friend and booster to everyone around her, visiting her widowed mother, going to church, and participating in some kind of volunteer work I really didn't care about. None of these activities seemed to me to be places where one could meet men—and, in any case, Babs didn't give off the air of someone who was really looking. She just seemed like a very, very nice girl. And we all know nice girls don't get dates.

I led Richard to Babs's table and introduced them. After I performed my two songs. I suggested we all go to a café around the corner.

It was clear in the café that Richard was really interested in Babs. When he went to the men's room, she confided to me that she liked him too—he was, in her words, a "Betty" (a word she'd coined for a cute guy even before it was used in *Clueless*).

Babs asked me if I had any interest in Richard. Because if I did, she told me, she wouldn't encourage him.

What a friend! I knew she meant it. I assured her that I had no interest in Richard beyond friendship.

Truthfully, I did feel a little jealous. Not because I felt Richard was my soul mate—I knew he wasn't—but because it's always hard, from an ego standpoint, to see someone who has rejected you take an interest in your friend. It was a feeling I had experienced before, and have many times since. But I never doubted that the right thing was to give Babs the "all clear"—and I was proud to be maid of honor at her and Richard's wedding.

At the time she met her future husband, although I was happy for Babs, the seeming injustice made no sense to me. It wasn't as if Babs had an extra shot of confidence. If anything, she lacked it. While she didn't go around feeling sorry for herself, she certainly didn't toot her own horn. Instead, she always seemed to make the people around her shine brighter.

How, I thought, could she attract her true love without trying, while I, who was doing everything that the women's-magazine gurus said to do if one wanted to land a husband, attracted only playboys?

The truth is, she *was* trying. She was completely open to meeting the right man—and she was trying every day to be the best human being she could be.

I don't think anyone could try harder than that—or with better results.

start me up:
how beginnings shape endings

Do you ever have one of those moments when you say some-thing that makes perfect sense to you, but the person you're address-ing has absolutely no idea what you mean?

It happened to me in late 2003, on one of my first dates after I began to get serious about chastity. I was saying good-bye to my date—also a believer—after we had what I thought was a pleasant lunch. It was our second time out together, and I hoped we would meet again. However, I became confused when he gave me what I thought were conflicting signals. He seemed to want to keep all his options open—not planning to see me again, but not ruling it out either.

I commented that, at that point in my life, I believed I should start every relationship as though it were going to resolve into marriage.

And I totally lost him.

I think it must have sounded as if I *intended* every relationship to end in marriage—which thankfully is not the case; otherwise, I'd get hurt a lot more often than I do.

I tried to explain to him that it involved not doing anything at the beginning of a relationship that I would later regret. Even if some tactic helps one win a mate, if it involves dishonesty, disrespect, playing games, or a lack of sexual restraint, it's not something one looks back on fondly after years of marriage.

In the New York City area where I live, whether men and women meet one another in bars, at work, through friends, or through the personals, the model for relationships remains the same for many: they become physically intimate to see if they want to be in a relationship.

That used to be my paradigm for a relationship too—the "Let's have fun and see if it turns into something" philosophy. The underlying concept is the old Freudian conceit that people have sexual "needs," and that these needs can exist either on their own or as the prelude to a relationship, but that it is unnatural to prioritize other types of intimacy ahead of them.

Although I myself do have these "needs"—or, rather, desires—I never *really* wanted to place them before emotional intimacy. I don't think it's natural for women to operate that way unless they have serious problems with emotional intimacy—and even then, I don't think it makes them happy.

Now that I'm no longer a hopeless fish in New York City's sea of singles, but instead a little Christian *ichthus* swimming against the current, self-restraint is a priority, as are the other things I mentioned earlier: honesty, respect, and not playing games. Those last three in particular seem obvious, but they go against the nature of dating in a sophisticated urban social world that encourages men and women to hide their true feelings from one another.

The example I should have given my date is that of drawing a circle. If someone asks you to draw a circle, and you agree, you don't get cagey and pretend at first that you're going to draw a square. It messes the whole thing up. If you're a woman of your word, you have to start the circle with the same steady curve with which it ends, because once you've started it, there's no way to go back and correct the beginning.

Likewise, it's practically impossible to draw a perfect circle without a compass, and it's impossible to start a relationship leading to marriage without a moral compass. In fact, without a compass, it's even harder to draw a perfect heart.

In 1973, during the height of the sexual revolution, Erica Jong's semiautobiographical best seller *Fear of Flying* popularized the notion of "zipless" sex. Calling it a "platonic ideal," the novel's heroine dreams of having sex with strangers in such a natural, flowing manner that she doesn't even notice the intruding sound of a zipper. Boy and girl would transition from meetup to hookup in a seamless, slippery slope.

I've rejected the notion of zipless sex—or, in the language of the Jong-inspired *Sex and the City*, having sex like a man—but that certainly doesn't mean I'm free from questionable platonic ideals.

Like Jong's heroine, my long-held fantasy involves meeting a stranger. I dream of beginning a relationship so smoothly and naturally that I don't do anything I'd regret. In this fantasy, my words and actions toward my new man are free from their usual awkwardness. I act with perfect wisdom and grace, without ever once stopping to second-guess myself. There are no embarrassing slips; you could even call it "slipless."

In reality, slipless meetings are just as unattainable as zipless encounters. Both fantasies stem from the quintessential fairy-tale image of being swept hopelessly off one's feet. A single moment of self-awareness would break the spell.

Being swept away means acting on impulse—something that, by its very nature, excludes the will.

In this day and age, when we picture what kind of decision we might have to make in a new relationship, we generally think in terms of whether the time is right to have sex. Romance, by contrast, is seen as something that must happen by itself—without a conscious decision. Any attempt to introduce an element of choice into it is seen as decidedly *un*romantic.

Whether your romantic ideal is zipless or slipless, the most obvious problem with relying on impulse is that it doesn't work. It didn't work for Erica Jong—she's on her fourth marriage as I write, the first three having ended in divorce. It certainly didn't work for me—and I've tried both zipless *and* slipless.

In fact, as soon as we buy into the idea that we "fall" in love, we're at a deficit. As noted psychologist Erich Fromm writes in *The Art of Loving*, the expression "falling in love" is misleading. "Falling" implies something one does accidentally, without even trying. Instead, Fromm writes, the experience should be called "standing in love," for it requires an act of will.

On some level, our culture—even with its emphasis on "falling"— is aware that love involves a decision. We speak of "opening up" our hearts to new loves, or we say a friend has "closed her heart" to an ex-boyfriend. We have a sense, however vague, that love involves the opening of a door.

There is indeed a door in the heart. Behind it is love that flows like a river. Its source is God—because God is love.

If we really love, we choose to open the door, making a conscious decision to admit the love we long to feel inside our hearts for one special man. The decision has to be conscious, because no matter how irresistible the attraction, we must choose whether or not to take on the responsibility of giving ourselves fully to another. We know that the love behind the door entails responsibility, because we know that it is for life.

Now, here's the exciting part. This great love to which we have access is meant to be shared in a sexual way with only one man—and that's for a reason.

God created marriage as a means to make us more like Him. The greatest way we can be like God is to love one another the way He loves us. In the words of Augustine, "God loves each of us as if there were only one of us."

In other words, God wants you to be able to love one man the way He loves you—as though you were the only person in the world. From there, He means to shape you further. In a deeply spiritual way, you're meant to spread the love that you share with your husband to the rest of the world.

This is why Christians believe that marriage is more than just a check box on the census form. It's a spiritual *vocation*. Those of us who long for it are called to it, in the same way that some people are called to be pastors.

The apostle John says of our relationship with God, "We love Him because He first loved us" (1 John 4:19 NKJV). Likewise, we are able to choose marriage because God chose us for marriage.

We publicly acknowledge our "yes" to marital love in our "I dos." The promises to love, honor, cherish, and obey, for richer or for poorer, in sickness and in health, forsaking all others, as long as we both shall live—these are the words tradition uses to remind us of the responsibilities contained within our assent. Yet, we know that the marriage vows are not really the beginning of our "yes."

C. S. Lewis wrote that those who get to heaven will realize, once they arrive, that they have in a sense always been there—that their experience of it began on earth.[11] Likewise, when you enter marriage, you will know that your "yes" to love began well before your "I do."

In the same way that arriving in heaven will cause those who are there to understand how heaven's seeds were planted long ago in their earthly lives, so, too, will being married bring you a deeper understanding of the nature of godly love. In the words of the apostle Paul, "being rooted and grounded in love, [you] may be able to comprehend with all the saints what is the width and length and depth and height—to know the love of Christ which passes knowledge; that you may be filled with all the fullness of God" (Ephesians 3:17–19 NKJV).

∽✺∾

The nature of marital love, enabling husband and wife to unite both spiritually and physically, not only is a symbol of God's love but *is* God's love. Symbolically, marital love is the image that appears in the Bible many times, from the Old Testament through the New, to show the intense love between the Lord and those who are called by His name. This is expressed beautifully in the Song of Solomon, when the bride says, "I am my beloved's, and my beloved is mine" (6:3 NKJV).

Yet, while marital love is meant to model God's love in a special way, it is by no means the only goal to which we are to aspire. This longing with which we are created, the desire to be complemented by another, has a purpose in and of itself. That purpose has deep meaning, enough to transform each one of us and—if we would follow it as far as it would lead us—everyone we touch.

As strange as it may seem, the purpose that sets our hearts afire and makes us long for marriage will not—in fact, *cannot*—be satisfied by setting marriage as our main goal. In fact, the single-minded pursuit of marriage will actually draw us farther away from completion and happiness.

That may sound like an odd assertion coming from one who believes fervently in the institution of marriage—and whose heart's desire is to be married. I am sharing it with you because, although it may sound on the face of it like a troublesome paradox, I am discovering in my own life that it is a liberating truth.

When I was a child, one of my favorite books was Lewis Carroll's *Through the Looking Glass*. At one point in that book, Alice sees the Red Queen and tries to walk over to her—only to discover that she's going the opposite direction. So she decides to take a different tack, walking *away* from the chess piece instead of toward her. Sure enough, within a minute, she finds herself face-to-face with the Red Queen.

Like Alice, I have a goal in mind. Mine is marriage. To fulfill it, I need to have a walk—a direction for my life. Yet, the more I walk in the direction of finding love, the farther I will be from my goal. That's because walking toward a mere object is not really a walk—it's a hunt.

A hunt, as we all know, generally winds up with something getting killed. If my object is love, the nature of the hunt means that once I find it, it's going to die. Only it won't die from a bullet; it'll die of starvation. No matter how much I may tell myself that I want to give all my love to a man, the hunter's mentality that I've bought into is centered around taking—not giving.

To be able to love, you have to give, and to be a true giver, you have to give to all—to both those who are close to you and those who aren't. "For if you love those who love you, what reward have you?" (Matthew 5:46 NKJV). There is a real reward in this life from giving without discriminating. It shapes you into the person God wants you to be.

As Charlie Kaufman wrote in his screenplay for *Adaptation*, "You are what you love, not what loves you."

This love is the moral compass that will enable you to both begin a relationship and bring it around to a perfect circle. The Greek word for it is *agape* (pronounced a-GAW-pay). It's the kind of love the apostle John meant when he wrote, "God is love" (1 John 4:8 NKJV). In the words of modern writer Peter Kreeft, "It means loving people not just in terms of justice or what they deserve, but simply loving them absolutely."[12] Forget falling in love or even standing in love—as Kreeft puts it, we *rise* in agape.

If you take that longing you feel in your heart and direct it toward sharing *agape* love with those around you, then you will never again have to worry about the million things that could go wrong in a budding relationship. None of those things will matter, because you will have a spark in your heart that will outshine all the externals. The man God has chosen for you will be drawn to that spark—and you'll see that same spark in him.

～∞〜

I used to think that hindsight was my enemy. Granted, if I paid heed to it—with its annoyingly perfect 20/20 vision—it could prevent me from making the same mistakes again. Most of the time, however, it just nagged at me—telling me everything I'd done wrong.

It was when looking back on relationships that hindsight proved especially maddening. To this day, I can look back at every first date that I had with a future boyfriend and see things I would have done differently—warning signs I missed, or missteps I made that would have grave consequences.

It gives me hope to realize that one day, when I am married to the man I love, hindsight will be my friend. I will be able to look back on my first date with him and recognize the seeds that would later blossom into love.

The best part of this new, improved hindsight is that I won't be looking back on some idealized first date where everything was perfectly smooth and "slipless." I'll be looking back at my real, (very) fallible self and my likewise-fallible future husband.

The difference is that I'll be looking through the eyes of love—and love covers a multitude of sins.

life beyond the "meet" market

I was in the living room of a condominium on the ninth floor of a posh Manhattan high-rise yesterday afternoon, as far east as you can get on the Upper East Side without falling into the East River. It was a baby shower for my newest friend, and there were many women I didn't know. While my pregnant pal was her usual welcoming self, I felt a bit out of place surrounded by so many upwardly mobile twenty- and thirty-somethings, with their long, straight hair and sleek Ann Taylor ensembles.

So, I struck up a conversation with the oldest woman there—my friend's mom—and mentioned I was writing a book for marriage-minded single women who'd had enough of the *Sex and the City* lifestyle. That perked up the ears of the Ann Taylor brigade. One of them leaned in my direction.

"But *how* do you meet men?" she asked plaintively.

Her eyes were sincere. Something in them reminded me of the story in Matthew's Gospel about the rich young man who came to

Jesus, asking what good thing he might do so that he might have eternal life.

When the man assured Jesus that he kept all the commandments, Jesus said, "If you want to be perfect, go, sell what you have and give to the poor, and you will have treasure in heaven; and come, follow Me" (Matthew 19:21 NKJV).

It wasn't the answer that the rich young man wanted; "he went away sorrowful, for he had great possessions" (v. 22 NKJV).

Likewise, I knew the woman at the shower wouldn't want to hear what I had to tell her. She had a lot invested in the idea of going out to certain places and doing certain things with the express purpose of meeting men. If I was going to be honest, I'd have to tell her to take her treasury of manhunting knowledge and chuck it out the window. It wouldn't buy her a marriage made in heaven.

∽∾

Chastity is a lifelong discipline, based on the understanding of the nature of sexual intimacy—what sex is and what it's for. Whether you practice chastity as a single woman (when it entails refraining from sex) or as a married woman (when it entails love and responsibility), it bears the same spiritual fruit.

If you come away from this book with only one message, let it be this:

Through chastity—and only through chastity—can all the graces that are part of being a woman come to full flower in you.

I have a floppy rubber tree that I keep by the window. Whenever I turn it, it reorients itself amazingly quickly—seemingly within a day—so that its leaves face the sunlight.

Now, imagine a plant prettier than my unwieldy rubber tree—a wildflower, growing in a field during summertime. This is a fable, so our wildflower has a mind of its own.

This flower, which is bathed in sunshine all around, decides it's not satisfied with the rays that are brightening its petals. It sets its desire on the sunlight that hits the opposite side of a nearby hill.

Every day, the flower strains toward the hill, trying in vain to reach the unreachable rays. As it points toward the distant light, ignoring the sunshine that's all around it, it contorts itself, bending farther and farther, until it's practically parallel to the ground.

Picture that for a moment.

That is a portrait of a woman who puts the goal of meeting a husband at the center of her thoughts, actions, and dreams.

She is forever leaning over, looking away, bringing herself down to point herself toward someone who *is not there*.

Think of the woman who, when she's speaking with a man at a party, is always turning her head to see if a more attractive man has walked in. I've caught myself doing that.

You might say, "But there *is* someone out there for me. It's not like I'm looking for a phantom."

I agree. God puts the longing for a husband in one's heart for a reason, and it's meant to be fulfilled. But orienting your whole perspective toward fulfilling that longing when the object of the longing is not in sight is like shooting blindly into the air, hoping you'll hit a duck. All it does is waste ammunition, annoy everyone within hearing distance, and destroy a few innocent sparrows.

Moreover, as even postfeminist dating manuals grudgingly admit, men like to do the hunting. A man may initially be excited by a woman who pursues him—and a shy one may well need encouragement—but he'll soon lose interest. He wants to feel as though the woman he's pursuing is a valuable prize. While he doesn't want her to play hard to get, winning her should bring him a sense of accomplishment. From that perspective, landing a woman who's built her life around finding a man is no great achievement.

The truth is that we don't need a distant light to give us hope to carry on. Like the wildflower in the summer field, whether we realize it or not, we have light all around us.

Chastity means working to be conscious of that light, absorbing it in our being so we may display our true beauty—like a flower in full bloom. There is love waiting for you—from your family, from your friends, from the strangers whose day you can brighten with your gifts of warmth and kindness. It's not far away. It's right here, right now.

∽∽

The world of comic-book fandom and *Star Trek* devotion has introduced a derisive new word into the language: "fanboy," with its lesser-used counterpart, "fangirl."

As I write, the online encyclopedia Wikipedia—to which anyone may contribute—says, "Fanboy . . . is a term used to describe a male who is utterly devoted to a single subject or hobby, often to the point where it is considered an obsession. The term originated . . . to describe someone who was socially insecure and used comics as a shield from interaction, hence the disparaging connotations."

A single woman who gets dating advice from *Glamour* and *Cosmopolitan*, goes to speed-dating events, keeps a condom in her purse "just in case," and barhops with a pack of heavily made-up female pals is, in my eyes, a fangirl. Like fanboys, she is socially insecure and uses a shield to protect herself from interaction. In the fangirl's case, the shield is emotional—a superficial exterior to protect herself from being vulnerable.

Remember the classic *Saturday Night Live* episode where William Shatner begged the fanboys at a *Star Trek* convention to "get a life"? "There's a whole world out there!" he cried. That's what I want to say to women whose minds are stuck on the "meet" market. I think that men—the good ones—want to say that to them too.

You can say that an obsession with finding a husband is more useful, more real-world, than an obsession with comic books or *Star Trek*. The desire for love and companionship is written in our hearts and souls. I'll be the first to agree. But there's a difference between having a desire and shaping all your longings around it.

We all want to make a living, but there are some people who are intent on moving up in their field. Whenever they go to parties or hang out with friends, they want to talk shop—whether it's the stock market, the media business, or whatever provides their paychecks.

I know lots of people in the journalism and entertainment worlds who are forever "schmoozing." They live for industry gossip—who's in, who's out. Whenever they call or send me an e-mail, I know they're going to ask for something—a phone number, a tip, any kind of "connection."

Such busybodies are, in a word, *annoying*. Sometimes they get what they want, because they're persistent, but they make lots of enemies along the way. Ultimately, they wind up envying others' success, unable to go as far as they'd like because they're seen as poseurs.

When a man with integrity—the kind of man you and I would like to meet—meets a fangirl in full husband-hunting mode, he reacts much the same way I do when Joe Poseur sweetly asks me for some editor's phone number.

Men don't like to feel used. They don't like to feel that a woman is interested in them only because she hears her biological clock ticking, or because she's desperately lonely, or because she has no life outside watching TV and getting drunk on the weekends.

Like attracts like. If you want a man who has strong values—one who's deep, wise, and trustworthy—you have to demonstrate strong values yourself. They have to be obvious in your every word, every action, every breath.

From my late teens through my twenties, rock and roll was my life. I wrote about it for publications like *Mojo* and Salon.com, and I spent several hundred evenings taking it in at sweaty, smoke-filled live-music nightclubs.

Although I genuinely loved music, a major reason for my immersing myself in the scene was that I thought musicians were the sexiest creatures on earth. I'd like to say it was because I was drawn to creativity and skill; indeed, I often went for talented songwriters. But then, I also pursued drummers, so there goes that theory.

The popular culture typically envisions rock stars as choosing one or more different groupies from a smorgasbord of possibilities each night. I don't doubt there really are stars like that. Such sexual compulsiveness was especially prevalent in the 1960s, when men and women shed their inhibitions amid the onslaught of the sexual revolution.

However, as I spent my share of time outside dressing-room doors, I discovered something that went against the common wisdom. The rockers who did the most touring were the least likely to spend the night with strangers. Instead, they would have a girl in every port—one woman to whom they'd return whenever they were in a particular town. Sometimes this woman would travel along with her rocker "boyfriend" for a few stops on a tour before parting ways until the next time the band came around.

These women weren't merely sex partners to their chosen musicians. When one of them met up with her special rocker, they looked to all appearances like a real couple—friends as well as lovers.

I understand now what I didn't understand then, which is the reason a man with no interest in monogamy, who could have his pick of women, would purposely limit his choices.

Men want home. Not just *a* home, but home—an indescribable feeling of being in a place where they are understood, where they belong, where they can rest in one woman's love. The desire for home is so strong that a man will keep trying to capture it even when his chosen lifestyle prevents him from achieving it.

So then, you may ask, if men want home, why don't the rockers I mentioned seek it in one woman, instead of having a girl in every port?

The answer lies in the nature of groupies. It's a feeling I know quite well, and it's not unique to women who follow rock stars. You'll find it, too, in the women's-magazine tales of ultradevoted girlfriends who mother their boyfriends, even baking and cleaning for them, only to be dumped.

A man feels loved only when he feels needed.

Groupies and other women who set out to mother men set themselves up as the giver in a relationship, so that all their boyfriend has to do is take. They suffer from a lack of self-esteem, so they sell themselves short. They long for their boyfriend to give of himself, but they live in fear that if they make such a request of him, he'll just move on to a less-demanding girlfriend.

If he's a rock musician, such fears are well founded; there's a good chance that, when faced with responsibility, he *will* move on. But when nothing's required of him, he won't stay long anyway— nor will he whittle down the number of his girlfriends to one.

You might completely, utterly, and desperately long for a man from the depths of your loins. But if you want him to be attached to you, you must require something of him in return. For a man to develop a bond, it's not enough that he's adored—he has to be appreciated.

For all the advances that the feminist movement has created for women in the working world, it's created terrible damage in what I consider the infinitely more important area of relationships. Women are told that self-sufficiency means refusing to allow men the opportunity to do things for them.

A good man does admire self-sufficiency in a woman. But he admires it even more when that self-sufficient woman has the modesty to admit she needs advice, a shoulder to lean on, or just someone to carry her loaded-down backpack.

∽✖✑∼

If you resist barhopping, casual sex, and other superficial foolishness that our culture tells us will lead to marriage, you're bound to have days when you wonder if it's worth it. After all, sometimes those things *do* lead to marriage. We all know someone who met her husband at a nightclub, a bar, or a booze-fueled party.

I think of people who haven't yet learned chastity as being like babies in the womb—unformed, incomplete, lacking a clear idea of the graces that could flower in them. When they marry, they're suddenly cast out into an unfamiliar world for which they're not ready. They're preemies.

Can such marriages succeed? Absolutely—but not without growing pains. Like premature infants, these newly marrieds have to work harder than fully formed individuals to conquer the hazards of their unfamiliar environment. And just as a premature birth may have ill effects on an infant for years to come, people who marry without understanding chastity are stunted. It will be hard for them to grow together as they should, because they have yet to develop spiritual gifts that are best nurtured before marriage—like patience, faithfulness, and self-control. Likewise, they will face greater challenges than chaste couples in deepening their spiritual bond, because they lacked depth at the outset.

This period of time when I'm a chaste single woman is my gestation. I strive to unite my will to God's, and I trust that He is forming me. I know that He is forming my future husband as well.

At the end of every day, even if it seems I'm no closer to meeting my husband, I know that I really am closer—because I'm closer to being the woman God wants me to be. When I'm "born" into marriage, the spiritual gifts I've developed will help me grow with my husband so that we'll develop our potential together.

The Bible's greatest love story, Song of Solomon, offers a picture of one in whom all the graces God grants to womanhood come to full flower. The glorious bride's intensely devoted love for her husband is meant to personify the church's love of Jesus. She is known as the Rose of Sharon.

There is a real plant called the rose of Sharon—a beautiful hibiscus. Appropriately enough, it's a late bloomer.

Solomon's bride is also called the lily of the valleys. Jesus observed in His Sermon on the Mount that God takes care of the lilies—they don't have to work. In the same way, He said, we should put our needs in God's hands:

"So do not worry, saying, 'What shall we eat?' or 'What shall we drink?' or 'What shall we wear?' For the pagans run after all these things, and your heavenly Father knows that you need them. But seek first his kingdom and his righteousness, and all these things will be given to you as well" (Matthew 6:31–33 NIV).

It's not about *how* you meet men. It's about *who* you are when you meet men. Take care of the "who," and the "how" will take care of itself.

That said, I can suggest a few good ways and means . . .

fourteen
join the club!

Well, the first thing to do, obviously, if you want to meet your future husband, is to get out of the house.

I say "obviously," knowing full well from experience that if you're lonely, that can be one of the hardest things to do. Going out alone because you have no one to go out with, only to be surrounded by seemingly happy couples, can take some serious stamina when you're keenly aware of your lack of a boyfriend. But if you've read this far, you know that what society tells you is a "lack" is nothing to be ashamed of. Moreover, the boldness and self-assuredness that you show in going out by yourself or with a female friend are qualities that the man you desire will find attractive.

Notice I wrote, "going out by yourself or with a female friend." The second thing to do if you want to meet your future husband is avoid going out in packs. It's fine to do it if all you want is a girls' night out. But if your intent is to put yourself in a place where the right man can find you, you can't be seen as part of a posse.

The reason to avoid packs is that they invite superficial behavior—

and the men who are drawn to them are superficial as well. A date of mine explained the pack mentality to me one Friday night as we walked through the streets of my city, which gets a heavy influx of young barflies.

My date observed that each of the packs of women hopping from one bar to another appeared to be led by one woman who was very attractive. This "alpha" woman was surrounded by her less-attractive friends, who seemed to hope that some of their pretty pal's cachet would wear off on them. Sure enough, once the pack hit a bar, the alpha would be surrounded, while her friends would perhaps get some attention from her failed suitors.

The vision sounds terribly cynical, but I don't doubt it's true for that kind of group, in that kind of circumstance. The kind of man who would approach a woman in a pack is usually—not always, but usually—one who is superficial, in that he sees a woman of a certain level of attractiveness and takes a chance to see if he can win her. He's also going to be a bit hard-nosed in thinking he can beat the competition.

The kind of man you and I want to meet is going to be daunted at the prospect of approaching a woman in a pack, because he'll be modest—not wanting to overestimate his ability to publicly compete for a prize. He'll also be deep, so he'll want to get to know his prospective date better than he could in a few minutes surrounded by others at a bar. And he'll be sensitive, not wanting to hurt the feelings of the other women by focusing his attention on one.

So, knowing that your best bet is to go it alone or with one female friend, once again, get out of the house! Are you reading this book at home? Don't! Take it with you to your nearest café, buy a cappuccino or a bottomless cup of coffee, and read it there. Any time you have reading to do after work, or at breakfast time, do it away from home—

if not at a coffee shop, then at a park where you feel safe. Likewise, use a safe place in public, away from home, to do any after-hours work you have, to study, or to surf the Internet.

It may feel weird at first to sit at a table for one, but you get used to it. If you go to the same place every day, the waiters and waitresses get to know you, and you feel at home. The advantages to getting out of the house in this way are fourfold:

- You run the chance of meeting a love interest or making a new friend;

- you get some social activity—even if it's just saying "hello" to the server who brings you your coffee;

- you become more confident, unafraid to be seen alone; and, last but not least,

- you get away from your television set.

I cannot overestimate the importance of that last point. It's bad enough that watching television can turn you into a couch potato. Worse, it feeds your brain a steady stream of images meant to keep you in a state of lack. According to TV, you can never be attractive enough or rich enough. You can never have enough sex. Most important, in TV's eyes, you can never have enough *things*.

Television advertisers crave single women in their twenties and thirties, because they watch more TV than married women and have a higher disposable income. As a result, such viewers are more likely to make impulse purchases and buy luxuries. You don't see too many married women blowing their Christmas bonus in the shoe department of Macy's.

In other words, you're worth more to television advertisers—

and, therefore, TV networks—as a single woman than as a married one. They have a vested interest in keeping you sitting in front of the tube like Bridget Jones, munching on potato chips and drinking Diet Pepsi in her PJs.

Television hates you.

Thankfully, there are many entertaining ways to escape the boob tube besides grabbing a solo espresso. Here are some of my favorites—all of them likely to put you in contact with interesting and eligible men:

- **Book clubs.** Reading groups or book clubs enable you to meet people in your area who share your literary interests. You will make acquaintances over an extended period of time as your group meets—usually once a week or once a month—to discuss the book you're all reading. There are book clubs for practically every interest—like mysteries, classics, romances, and religious literature—and they often attract intelligent, articulate participants.

  You can find book clubs in your area through a phone call to your local library or bookstore. Houses of worship often have book clubs as well, as do coffeehouses, student unions, and community centers.

  To meet people your age, look for book clubs that meet in or near universities, or that are led by someone your age, or that cover books that appeal to your age-group. (For example, if you're in your twenties, you probably don't want to join a book club that's reading *Tuesdays with Morrie*, Mitch Albom's best seller about his meetings with an old, dying college professor.) Also, look for clubs that don't make you pay in advance to attend several meetings. That way, if you go to one meeting and find that there's no one there to whom you can relate, you won't be stuck with an unwanted membership. Most book clubs that I've found don't charge a fee at all.

My own book-club experience lasted a couple of years (until my newspaper job had me working nights). I belonged to the New York City Chesterton Society, which read the works of my favorite religious author, G. K. Chesterton. We met in the apartment of a delightful ex-monk who would make us cappuccino or pour beer into majestic brass flagons for us as we discussed the finer points of our reading selection. I didn't get any dates out of the group, but I enjoyed the meetings so much and made such great friends that I kept going just for the fellowship.

I found the Chesterton reading group through the Web site of the American Chesterton Society, www.chesterton.org. Many other authors' Web sites also list reading groups for their fans, or have bulletin boards where readers may connect with one another.

- **Sports clubs.** Love running? Lucky you! The most running I do is to catch the subway train, which is too bad, because women who enjoy running have many excellent opportunities to meet men who share their passion. There are seven hundred running clubs around the country—with some 175,000 members—listed on the Road Runners Club of America Web site, www.rrca.org. To join them, you don't have to be a pro by any means; many Road Runners clubs accept members at any pace. As with book clubs, it's a great way to get to know people over an extended period of time. Unlike book clubs, it enables you to do so chastely while getting all hot and sweaty. Clubs for other kinds of sports, like cycling, are great too. You can often find out about them from your local Y or other health club.

- **Church-sponsored social groups.** There are two kinds of church-sponsored social groups. One is indispensable if you're trying to meet men who share your faith—and the other should be avoided at all costs.

The wrong kind is one of those that my pastor aptly describes as "young-adult groups that are neither young nor adult." It focuses its activities around drinking, seeing the latest R-rated movies, and going on "retreats" that are really just weekend-long parties. All right, maybe that *does* sound exciting—if you like the idea of turning your church basement into a sort of "Animal House" with crosses.

For example, as I write this, I am looking at the Web site of a New York City "contemporary" Christian young-adult group advertising its "monthly happy hour for those in their 20s: There will be $5 mixed-drink specials, and $3 beers."

The fact that the event benefits a food pantry doesn't alter its nature—drinking is drinking, whether it's for a good cause or not. There's nothing uniquely Christian about attending an event like this; you may meet people of faith there, but you can't expect them to act out their faith in such an environment. The free-flowing booze invites them to treat one another just as they would in a singles bar -as objects.

As if to drive home the point, the same young-adult group also has an upcoming "Extreme Charity Pub Crawl."

The right kind of church social group focuses not on booze and bars, but on faith and fellowship. That's where you'll meet men who are of stronger moral fiber than Joe Chug-It at the Last Chance Saloon. It's a group like the one to which my blogger pal Mike "Nightfly" (nightfly.blogspot.com), a single, chaste man in his mid-thirties, belongs—and that I'd join if it weren't fifty miles away—YACHT: Young Adult Christians Hanging Together.

The name says it all: YACHT hangs together through its members' supporting one another, doing things that enable them to get to know one another in a safe, warm, and supportive environment. Every two weeks, they meet at a local restaurant for "Bible study, faith sharing, and socializing." The "socializing" includes drinking—but it's clear from the event's description that the alcohol only supplements the fellowship; it's not the main attraction. (A person who's just out to get drunk isn't likely to go to an event advertised as a Bible study.)

The YACHT members often go to movies and plays—as long as they're not heavy on sex and violence—and go on sightseeing trips. About once a month, they do a "service project"—a volunteer effort aimed at helping the needy in their community. They also have frequent get-togethers in members' homes, like potluck dinners or game nights, where they duke it out at cards, Scrabble, Monopoly, and the like.

Belonging to a group such as YACHT makes you feel like part of a family—and when you're living chastely, you need the spiritual sustenance an extended family can provide.

- **Young Democrats/Young Republicans/Libertarians/etc.** Speaking purely in terms of volume, not quality, I have gotten more dates out of political social groups than any other kind of social outing. In fact, in the past few years, I've probably gotten more dates out of such groups than everything else *combined*. In general, men tend to be more politically active than women. At gatherings that cater to a particular political party, you're almost certain to find yourself part of a small and precious female minority.

But before you get on the Internet and track down your local political party's youth wing, beware. More dates also means more duds.

As with churches' neither-young-nor-adult groups, the operative word for many of these political-party social groups is "party." As a result, they attract many men who are just looking to score. Some of these men are smooth and handsome, pursuing intelligent women who will listen to them speak convincingly about political issues. At best, however, such smooth operators are just serial monogamists—men who can be faithful for a time, but who ultimately run away from commitment. (Bitter? Me? Ha!)

On the really low end of the spectrum, some men will purposefully attend events of political groups with which they disagree, just because they've heard the women there are "easy." I knew a conservative/libertarian law student who attended Socialist Party functions incognito for that very purpose. As if that's not scummy enough, he would then write about his Commie conquests on his blog. Some other good-looking men I saw at conservative functions, were secretly members of the left-wing Billionaires for Bush. To this day, I'm not sure whom they were fooling—the conservatives or the Billionaires.

Now that you've been thoroughly warned, be prepared to have a lot of fun at political social-groups' events. They usually have a monthly meeting with a featured speaker—a journalist, political expert, or local politician—followed by drinks or dinner at a nearby watering hole. Some people skip the meeting and just go for drinks, but I'd advise going to the meetings too; that's a good way to tell which men are there for the politics and which are there for the partying. Men with integrity, who are seriously interested in what's going on in the world, will attend the meeting and be impressed to see an intellectually engaged woman there as well.

If you do go to a political social group's meeting and get attention from a man—and more than one are likely to notice you during your first time there—take it slow. I'm not advising this just for the sake of chastity (though that's reason enough), but rather to give you time to learn the contours of your new social environment.

After all, if you really care about politics, chances are you'll want to continue to attend the meetings. You don't want to rush into something with a regular member of the group, only to have it not work out and then have to face that member at future meetings. It's better to get to know the group's members over the course of two, three, or more meetings, watching how they socialize and discovering whether they're genuinely interested in what you have to say—or if they're just scouting the room for possible dates. Do that and you may well bypass the duds to find a dream.

- **Team-trivia games.** I know, I know, I've been going on about the dangers of bars like a Prohibition crusader in overdrive. But there is *one* thing I've discovered in bars that is a great way to meet brainy, witty, and—sometimes—seriously desirable men: the team-trivia game.

I'm not talking about Trivial Pursuit or the video-trivia setup that some bars have. There's a newer kind of trivia game that's caught fire in the last few years, in which a real live human—not a video—calls out questions in a variety of categories, and teams of players write down the answers. At the end of the game, the answer sheets are graded and the teams with the most right answers win prizes. It's sometimes called Quizzo—like the popular one in Philadelphia (www.quizzo.com). By any name, it's the only way I know that one can instantly become popular in a bar for one's mind, not for one's looks.

If this all sounds terribly nerdy, it may not be for you, but I know from experience that people who play team trivia week after week make new friends—and, sometimes, meet their mate.

My friend Valerie is no geek by any means—she's a hip, street-savvy New Yorker—but when she went to Tuesday Night Trivia, she fell in love with one of the star players. Jon, a journalist and copy editor, was a classic diamond in the rough: a looker handicapped in the dating game by thick glasses and a shy, self-effacing manner. Today, they're newlyweds—and they made a beautiful couple on their wedding day (even more so with Jon sporting brand-new contact lenses).

- **Start your own club.** I've started a number of successful social groups and events—from Tuesday Night Trivia, to a DJ dance night, to a cocktail hour for people in the media—and there's one thing I've learned: if you call something a "club," people will immediately want to join. You know what they say about life being like high school with money? It's true. Just as in high school, *nobody* wants to be left out of a club.

  Another advantage to starting a club is that inviting a love interest to one of your club's events gives you an opportunity to get to know him better with other people around. There's less pressure on you both if he comes to the event than if you're out on a one-on-one date; plus you'll see a social side of him that you wouldn't see if you were alone with him. Also, if you're not sure whether he's romantically interested in you, you can invite him to one of your club's events without its seeming as though you're asking him on a date.

Starting your own club may or may not bring you in contact with new men—it could be that just the same few friends turn up at each meeting—but it will provide fun and fellowship in the meantime. Here are a few ideas to get you going. You start by inviting your friends, friendly acquaintances, and chummy coworkers—and then let them invite their friends:

Gourmet club: A group that meets regularly (every Wednesday, for example, or the first Wednesday of the month) to try out a new restaurant at the upper end of the clubgoers' price range. (It can't be *too* pricey, though; you don't want to scare people off.) Members agree to order as a group—sharing the dishes and splitting the bill—to get a fuller impression of the restaurant's menu. The sharing also invites conversation, making it easier for members to get to know one another.

Salon: About twenty years ago, some hipster got the idea of reviving an old-fashioned notion: invite a group of friends to your home, serve them coffee, discuss a particular topic—like political issues of the day, philosophy, or faith—and call it a "salon." Bingo! Suddenly, it's cool to just sit around and talk.

Movie club: Do you or a friend have a large-screen TV? Pick a favorite genre of film—like romances, thrillers, or Disney classics—and screen a film from that genre for the club on a regular basis. If you need ideas, the American Film Institute has compiled a number of lists, from "America's 100 Greatest Movies" to the "100 Funniest Comedies" and "100 Greatest Love Stories"; you can find them online at www.filmsite.org/afi100films.html. Each club member should bring a different refreshment to share with the rest of the group, so that there's a delicious variety of movie treats.

- **Volunteering.** You've probably already read that volunteering is an excellent way to meet eligible men, and for good reason. For one thing, it gives you an opportunity to learn about your fellow volunteers while working alongside them, learning more about their character than you would from a casual meeting. For another, it puts you alongside men who share your desire to help others, and who have other qualities that are important in a husband—like integrity, kindness, and generosity.

It's the part about sharing your desire to help others that's the kicker. If you want to meet men through volunteering, you've got to want in your heart to make the world—or some small part of it—a better place. Otherwise, you won't be at your best if an attractive man comes along while you're volunteering, or you'll tire too quickly if one doesn't come along.

Most of the volunteering I've done has been more one-on-one (like delivering meals to homebound seniors), but my friend Caren Lissner—a novelist (*Carrie Pilby*) who started Tuesday Night Trivia with me—often does volunteer activities that involve a larger group. "One thing to do is to volunteer with a friend," she advises, "because sometimes you might show up for an activity and not even get a volunteer job; the people running volunteer activities are often as harried as the volunteers and the people they serve. They do need volunteers, but sometimes things can get hectic. Of course, there are plenty of activities you can do alone, and sometimes being alone makes it easier to talk to other volunteers and get to know them.

"There are so many volunteer opportunities that it's good to find one that will interest you and open new worlds," Caren adds. Many of these opportunities are listed on Web sites or in newsletters by groups called volunteer clearinghouses or service corps. A phone call to your state governor's office, or a Web search for your state and "volunteer clearinghouse" should connect you with your local service corps. These organizations make it easy for busy young professionals to find opportunities to give a few hours here and there. Chances are that whatever your interests—comforting babies, aiding seniors, caring for animals, or helping the environment, to name a few—there's a volunteer opportunity in your area that would enrich your life.

Caren recommends volunteering with Habitat for Humanity (online at www.habitat.org), a nonprofit that builds homes for low-income families, "because you are working alongside other adults and really have the time to talk and get to know them." Habitat for Humanity builds at sites throughout the United States as well as overseas, and you can volunteer for as little as one day to see how you like it.

"Soup kitchens are another way to get to know people among the handing out of food and waitering and everything else," Caren adds. "Usually the volunteers eat some of the food together before the meal."

If you start volunteering, you may well discover—as Caren and I have—that the rewards are greater and more varied than you expected. "Remember that any event that shapes your personality and makes you a richer human being will add to your ability to find someone and to relate to different types of men and women in the future," Caren says. "There is always something gained by a new experience, besides the good you do in the world by giving to others."

fifteen
clothes encounters

When I first set chastity as a goal, my bed got the message way before my closet. My new lifestyle gave me a new kind of confidence—and I associated confidence with showing off my body in sexy clothes.

From adolescence and even earlier, young women are taught to use makeup and clothing as a shortcut to self-worth. They learn that with help from the makeup-counter saleswoman, they can achieve a more "mature" look that makes them stand out from their classmates. They learn that they can instantly become more popular with boys just by wearing high heels.

It's natural for girls to want to experiment with ways to dress themselves as they make the transition into womanhood. What's sad is that our culture, through the media—particularly women's magazines—tries to keep women in a girlish emotional state.

When it comes to self-image, makeup and clothing should be, at best, a crutch—good for a pick-me-up, but not for a psychological foundation. Women should be taught early on that, as Jesus said, the body is more important than clothes.

I used to see my clothing as part of a chemical formula, of sorts: Take me; add heavy makeup; a low-cut, thigh-baring dress, and knee-high black leather boots; and ka-boom! Instant male reaction.

Even though I knew the reaction was to my revealing clothes and not to my personality, I didn't mind because I preferred to get any reaction over none at all. I feared that if men didn't notice my body right away, I would be invisible to them. Wearing clothes and makeup that were guaranteed to get noticed, then, gave me a sense of control.

Needless to say, once I became chaste, my old ways of dressing were a recipe for disaster. I quickly discovered that chaste woman plus unchaste clothing equals instant hypocrite.

I may have known what was in my heart, but others around me didn't. To them, I looked like a phony. It's for reasons like this that the apostle Paul said to avoid all appearance of evil (see 1 Thessalonians 5:22 KJV).

At the same time that I was unintentionally misleading others, I was fooling myself. No matter how confident I was in my chastity, the way I dressed unquestionably affected my behavior. I would conduct myself in a different way if I wore pumps and a minidress that hugged all my curves—it was "the iniquity of my heels" all over again.

Eventually—after some pretty awkward times trying to dress one way and act another—I realized what was the problem. I was treating chastity as if it were merely a lifestyle choice when, as with marriage, it's far more than that. It's a *vocation*.

"Vocation" isn't a term one hears much in conversation. When it is used, it usually means something having to do with a job. In fact, a vocation is much more than a nine-to-five. It's a mission.

We choose to work at our jobs. We choose to *become* our vocations.

Notice I said "choose." The beauty of a vocation is that it is a choice. When we choose it, as with choosing chastity, we take charge of our circumstances and thereby open the doors to all manner of blessings—gifts we could never receive if we looked at our state in life as something merely forced upon us.

For example, look at the vocation of motherhood. Some mothers with young children always seem to be uncomfortable around their kids. They seem unable to control the little ones or enjoy them. Other mothers take a natural delight in their kids. They know how to keep the unruly ones in line without losing their tempers. The first kind of mom views motherhood as a job; the second, as a vocation.

Once I began to view chastity as a vocation, I wanted to dress in a way to suit my vocation. This was much different from the way I'd changed my wardrobe in the past, when I'd upgrade it for a new job. I had to completely rethink the way I dressed not only at work but everywhere I went.

Was it depressing to chastitize my wardrobe? Only if you think being a Hollywood star is depressing.

It's ironic, I know—Hollywood isn't particularly known for its chastity—but the best example of dressing to suit one's vocation is the way stars dress to suit their vocation. I'm not saying to go out and do a "Pretty Woman" shopping spree on Rodeo Drive. Rather, look at the way stars view their identities.

A beautiful Hollywood movie actress is a Hollywood movie actress *all the time*. She can never leave her house in just any old rag. She has to be fashionable at every moment, because heaven forbid the paparazzi catch her sunning herself in last year's swimsuit.

The actress dresses as a star 24/7 partly because she knows that having a fashionable public image will help her get good roles. But she also does it because it's expected of her. She is a star; therefore, her public wants her to look like a star. The actress fulfills the public's expectations because she loves being a star and has freely chosen that life.

That's what it's like to have a vocation. You choose a role in life and you remain true to it in your actions and appearance even if there are some mornings when you'd rather be someone else. You do it because you know that your dedication and hard work will pay off—both in the short term and in the long term.

Like a star, you step onto a stage every time you leave your doorstep. Your public is everyone you meet during the course of the day—from neighbors to coworkers, friends, and strangers. To them, your vocation of chastity includes a ministry—a ministry of beauty.

I actually think that chaste women have a greater responsibility than unchaste women to look good. By dressing in a way that reveals our natural grace without exploiting our bodies, we can radically affect the world—cutting through the superficiality and showing that beauty is more than skin-deep.

After all, a chaste single woman who dresses beautifully has no agenda. She's not trying to manipulate you with her sexiness, nor is she trying to win your sympathy with her plainness. She is modestly sharing all the gifts—both physical and spiritual—that God gave her. In this way, she flies in the face of a culture that refuses to acknowledge any motive a person might have for beauty other than personal gain.

My rules are simple. When I'm picking out an outfit, I ask myself if it makes me the slightest bit self-conscious about my body. Now, I don't mean, "Does it make me wish I were thinner?" I can put on just about any outfit and wish my rear end were smaller, my stomach flatter, and so on.

I mean, for example, if I'm trying on a skirt, I ask myself honestly,

"Am I going to feel like people are just staring at my thighs?" If my instincts say yes, then my instincts are probably right—it's better to find a well-styled skirt that leaves a little more to the imagination. Likewise, if I'm trying on a blouse, I ask myself, "When I walk into a room, are people's eyes going to be automatically drawn to my chest?" Again, if the answer's yes, I'm better off with a blouse that is in my favorite color and fabric but not quite as tight or low-cut.

A great thing to do is go through your closet, take out anything that doesn't fit you perfectly, and donate it to your local thrift store. There's no reason to own anything ill fitting. It's depressing, plus it leaves the uncomfortable possibility that you might try to squeeze into a too-tight skirt when everything else is in the laundry.

Many women who believe they are overweight try to hide their bodies in clothes that are too big. If that's you, please, give the extra-large sweatshirts to the Salvation Army and spend some quality time in Lane Bryant. There are so many attractive, well-tailored clothes for large-size women now—many more than when I was a 172-pound, size 18 college student—that you shouldn't deprive yourself of a chance to feel prettier.

Some types of clothing are clearly out if you're living the chaste vocation—like heels so tall and uncomfortable that you wobble in them, anything patent vinyl other than raincoats, and underwear-as-outerwear. But unless you're contractually obligated to wear a corset in broad daylight, you're probably not going to miss any of those things once you get used to chaste dressing.

I wear skirts varying from knee-length to mid calf—still sneaking in the occasional mini, but without coupling it with crocheted tights and a low-cut top as I used to do. I wear lots of velvet in the winter, and patterned cotton in the summer. It seems as though practically every time I go to the thrift store, I come back with another 1960s cocktail dress. I have boot-cut jeans that fit, and boots to wear with them. And of course, living in the New York City area, I wear *way* too much black.

In short, I'm having far too much fun indulging my clothes-horse sensibilities to miss the prechastity, black- patent-vinyl, hot-pants jumpsuit (straight out of the Sixties sci-fi film *Barbarella*) that I tossed into the trash. More than that, I feel truly confident that I'm both looking my best and projecting the image of a capable, secure, and dynamic woman.

As a kid, I thought my mother looked like Shirley Jones of TV's *The Partridge Family*, and her wardrobe was every bit as groovy. The first article of clothing that I can ever remember wanting desperately to wear was Mom's purple ankle-length halter-dress. Later on, during the early 1980s, she had a very cool *Private Benjamin*–style zippered army jumpsuit, and later still, I was thrilled when she gave me her tiered brown velvet skirt.

Because Mom has a love of fashion as well as an understanding of chastity, I asked her to share her thoughts on how changing one's image can help change one's life. Here's what she said:

Imagine a lighted Christmas tree, set up in your living room, two weeks before Christmas. Underneath are presents of all shapes and sizes in abundant array. All of them are wrapped carefully in colorful paper. Some glitter, some have a quieter beauty. There are beautiful bows on some. Some have curly ribbon, some have funny stickers. You don't know what is inside any of them. You know some of the things you have asked for, some of the things you have wished for. But you also like surprises. You imagine what is in some of the presents, but you are not sure. You hope that one gift, at least, will knock your socks off. And one gift will be the gift you have imagined only in your dreams.

Now, imagine the same tree, with only a few presents still wrapped. Even those have been handled. Some of the wrapping paper is ripped and the ribbons are untied. But most of the presents are open a little, so you can peek inside. You know that this one has a CD player (not the brand you asked for); this one is a sweater (not your best color); this one is a crystal vase (just another thing to dust). You know you will use a lot of these gifts. You also will give some away to the Salvation Army. One or two are things you asked for. But the magic of the wrappings is gone, and none of the gifts knock your socks off, none are the gifts of your dreams. You are thankful, but it's a "same old, same old" Christmas.

God made you to be a gift for the world. Part of being a gift is in the packaging. You look best when you are packaged as a surprise. You look worst when you have been shop-handled.

This is all about modesty, the right kind of modesty. Modesty is not looking like a church mouse. Modesty is looking like a wonderful gift.

With her analogy of the Christmas presents, Mom brings up a great point: modesty is sexy! Men have notoriously vivid imaginations—and they enjoy exercising them. Wearing modest but pretty clothes builds an air of mystery around you. To a man who finds you the least bit attractive, the fact that you clearly value your body, yet don't wish to display too much of it, is tantalizing. It suggests to him that what you're hiding is at least as attractive as what he can see.

But modesty, as my mother suggests, is not merely to awaken curiosity in the opposite sex. That would reduce it to the level of a commodity. In fact, modesty is part of the chaste way of life, a vocation that should affect how we relate to everyone—not just potential boyfriends.

When I think of living out the vocation of chastity, I think of Jesus's words: "For everyone who has will be given more, and he will have an abundance. Whoever does not have, even what he has will be taken from him" (Matthew 25:29 NIV). Those who are concerned only with pleasing a small group of people—like single women who care only about how they look to men—are living as though they have very little to give. Because they define themselves by their lack, and ration out their kindness as though there were a famine, what little happiness they have will be taken away from them.

The chaste woman who lives out her vocation is acting to all around her as though she has an abundance of loving-kindness. I say "acting" because she may not always feel terribly loving—yet she steps out in faith to give of herself, trusting that God will accept her sacrifice of kindness and make it into a thing of beauty. Because she is living on the principle that she has something to give, she "will be given more," and will indeed "have an abundance."

∽◦⌇◦∾

My mother got her own love of fashion from her mom—my beloved grandma Jessie. Grandma was so beautiful as a child that when her brothers and sisters used to reenact movies in their backyard, she always got to play the lead roles—because they all loved dressing her up. I remember how much she adored accessories; as a kid, I used to play with her fancy gloves and costume jewelry.

When I asked Mom for her thoughts on modesty, she closed them with a memory from Grandma's last days. It touches me to read it, because I remember how sick my grandmother was for months on end, and how it seemed that nothing could make her smile. With Grandma gone, Mom's words remind me that it is such a blessing to be able to share inner and outer beauty—especially with people who don't have enough of it in their lives:

I remember when my mom was in the hospital, dying of a dreadful disease. She could hardly move or talk. Unlike most of the hospital visitors, I did not wear jeans and a sweatshirt to see my mom. I dressed up. I was clean and sparkling, with makeup on. I looked like I was going out to a show. My mom's eyes lit up when she saw me: "You look beautiful!" Reviving my mom's spirits during those hospital visits, I realized that I was created to celebrate. In fact, I am to be a celebration for the world!

sixteen
crush and burn:
dealing with temptation

When I was nine, I was in the "boys are not all yucky, and I kind of like some of them" stage. It's a very nice stage to be in, and I recommend it. Much easier to take than the ensuing "obsessed with boys" stage, and far more pleasant than the preceding "boys are just yucky" stage.

Unfortunately, nine is a very difficult age to care about what boys think of you, because it's also an age when you're liable to lose teeth. When I was at summer camp that year, my smile had a big gap that made any attempts at glamour look ridiculous.

Despite the hole in my grin, I couldn't stay away from the object of my attraction, a wisecracking twelve-year-old named Jason Brimer. I always liked boys who made me laugh, and he was unquestionably the camp clown, with his celebrity impressions and practical jokes.

Jason must have known that I liked him, because I wasn't terribly subtle in trailing him around the campground. But beyond that, I knew I couldn't hope for much. He was far too popular to make time for a goofy little squirt like me.

One morning, I was awakened by the sound of shouting. The boys were raiding our cabin! I looked down from my top-bunk bed to find the room swarming with boys making noise, throwing things around, and generally wreaking havoc.

The first thing I did was pull up my blankets as high as I could while still peeking out. The long-sleeved polyester nightgown I'd worn to bed had gotten hot during the night and I'd slipped it off under the covers. God forbid the boys should discover I was *naked*!

Pretending to be coolly oblivious to the mayhem around me, I waited anxiously for the shouting, shampoo squirting, and panty throwing to end.

But I couldn't fool Jason Brimer.

He strolled up to the edge of my bed, which was at about the level of his nose. I quaked a little as he looked up at me. My big fear was that I'd be exposed. *Please, God, don't let him pull down my bedspread!* But even if that didn't happen, Jason might still destroy me with his wit. I got called names all the time, but an insult from him would really hurt.

He smiled. I shyly started to smile back.

"Hi, toothless," he said. Then he ran away.

Afterward, as my bunkmates and I put the personal effects that the boys had strewn about back into our cubbyholes, a girl who had seen Jason come up to me asked what had transpired.

When I told her, she said, "Wow, he must not like you."

"No," I said bravely. "He *does* like me. He said it because he can't say he likes me." (It is not for nothing that I am a psychologist's daughter.)

My hope was borne out mere days later, when Jason gave me a quick kiss—on the neck, no less. I gleefully told a counselor—who immediately cornered Jason, and that was the end of *that*. But that's not what matters.

What matters is that, for the rest of my life, whenever I find myself slipping back into a "boys are yucky" mode, I will remember the sheer joy of that "Hi, toothless."

In a moment, in a room full of people who are talking loudly and carrying on, one man can say two words that create a startling, tantalizing, utterly delicious feeling of intimacy. It's happened to me since my summer-camp days, and I know it'll happen again. However, if it does occur in a room full of people, I think it's safe to say I *won't* be naked in bed.

$$\infty$$

As a woman, sudden attention from an attractive man can cause instantaneous, delightful changes in your mind and body. That's why, when you're practicing chastity, the first thing to understand about temptation is that if you're *not* vulnerable to it, you're doing something wrong.

I don't mean to go out and look for temptation—far from it. Just as we ask God, "Lead us not into temptation," so we should avoid it—including avoiding people, places, and situations that are liable to tempt us.

To understand what I'm saying, look back at the reasons why you first considered chastity. If you're like me, years of casual flings and dead-end relationships left you disappointed, cynical, jaded, burned out—or all of the above. Sure, I could still get infatuated with a new man, but after being hurt so much, I often doubted I could maintain a mature love relationship—let alone a lifetime marriage.

For those of us who have had premarital sex, one of the main purposes of chastity is not just to become pure, but to become *new*. It requires a regeneration of the heart, so that we are no longer chained to old behaviors, but instead walk in "newness of life." To live out one's chastity, it's essential to shed one's disappointment, lose that protective shell of cynicism, and walk as though experiencing the world for the first time. It means returning to the way you were when men were a source of surprise and delight—those "Hi, toothless" moments.

Being as new doesn't mean losing wisdom gained over the years about the ways of the world. It means being in this world but not of it; knowing what is in darkness, while living in the light.

One thing that being as new *doesn't* mean is being "re-virginized" or a "born-again virgin." The very idea of being a born-again virgin implies that one's past is so shameful that one must whitewash it, rewriting history like a Communist textbook author.

As long as you've repented of your past behavior—turning away from it and resolving not to repeat it—you have nothing to be ashamed of. When we bring everything we've done before God, He can take even our mistakes and make them work out for good, granting us the insight to learn from them.

Once you become a new creation, fully open to whatever blessings are in store for you, you begin to be spiritually ready to meet your future husband. As usual, however, the devil is in the details. That very openness to blessings is precisely what makes you vulnerable to temptation.

Being tempted, in and of itself, is not wrong; only acting on it is. Moreover, even if you do act on temptation, you have much to gain by stopping yourself—no matter how far you've gone.

Our culture encourages an all-or-nothing mentality. You opened that bag of M&Ms even though you're on a diet? Might as well eat the whole thing—your diet's blown. An alcoholic has one drink after being dry for a month? She might as well get drunk—she's "off the wagon."

When it comes to sex, the defeatism is compounded by an ingrained cultural attitude that a woman has to finish what she starts, or else she's a tease. Men, of course, know this; a cad will prey upon a woman's fear that he'll accuse her of leading him on. At those times when it's hard to retain a clearheaded perspective, it helps to remember that there is *never* a point of no return.

The road to temptation, far from being black-and-white, is a continuum that leads to ever-darkening shades of gray. That can make it difficult sometimes to gauge when one has slipped onto it, especially when initially meeting someone. You may accept a man's invitation for a dinner date, only to discover that he thinks it's going to be a dinner-and-back-to-my-place date. But while it's always possible to progress farther away from chastity, it's also always possible to stop wherever you are—and know you'll have a shorter trip back than if you continue.

I came to my senses once while half-naked on a date's couch. As I described earlier, I told my bewildered date, Bill, that I was spitting in God's face by brazenly thinking I could have sex with a man He hadn't chosen for me. Then I put my clothes back on, excused myself, and left.

I'm sure Bill thought I was some kind of fanatic; the look in my eyes as I suddenly tore myself away from him must have been pretty intense. In leaving his apartment the way I did, I took the chance that he might be spiteful and tell his male friends to stay away from me.

I don't know if Bill actually blabbed to his buddies, but if he did, he was ultimately doing me a favor. You never have to fear if a playboy is spreading rumors that you're a prude. Chances are that a gossipy guy who sleeps around doesn't even know a decent man—and if one happened to overhear him, he'd consider the messenger.

Although one always has to be on guard for outright seducers, I found that when I first began practicing chastity, my strongest temptations came from much subtler sources. They were men with whom I already had a connection: ex-boyfriends, long-distance flames, or "passionate friends."

When you've been available to a man in the past—especially a man who's "on-call," a not-quite-boyfriend who hooks up with you when you're both lonely and between relationships—it's very hard to explain to him why you're no longer available. I know because I had just such a flame, and ending my sexual relationship with him was messy.

"Jay" was boyishly handsome, polished, and intelligent, with pale blue eyes. (I am a sucker for pale blue eyes.) He and I had never enjoyed what I would call a real relationship—one where both people live in the same time zone. We met through mutual friends, and, for the entire time we'd known each other, we had always lived three thousand miles apart. Our chemistry was good on the rare occasions when we'd find ourselves in the same town, but we both knew it wasn't strong enough to make one of us move closer to the other.

Despite the lack of intensity, over the course of ten years, Jay and I felt increasingly comfortable with each other—even though we'd had only about a dozen dates. Most times, we didn't sleep together; we'd just catch up over dinner and exchange some passionate kisses. I never really felt I knew him—he was reserved, and anyway, you can't really get to know someone at such a distance—but the bit of his personality that he showed me was warm and nonjudgmental.

It was because Jay didn't judge me that I had such a hard time, on our last date, explaining why I couldn't kiss him anymore—or do anything else physical with him, for that matter. (It didn't help that, by then, I had already kissed him hello.)

When you're faced with a situation like that, where you have to defend your chastity to a onetime sex partner, the best thing to do is state it simply and not apologize. With Jay, I said, "From now on, I'm saving myself for my husband, because all the kissing and all the sex I ever had never led to marriage."

There is something about the words "I'm saving myself for my husband" that tend to close the door on further conversation. Jay didn't press me too much after that.

He also couldn't argue with my logic. Even if he countered by asking how I knew chastity would lead to marriage, it was obvious that kissing *him* wouldn't bring me any closer to a wedding ring.

As I said, it was messy; Jay responded with a noticeably bitter "Do what you have to do" kind of comment. I don't think I'm on his list of potential Manhattan dinner partners anymore. But it doesn't matter—because I can look at myself in the mirror and know that I did the right thing.

Every time you overcome temptation, you put yourself in line for a reward. My reward for asserting my chastity to Jay was peace of mind. I realized that by being honest and straightforward with him, I showed him more respect than I had ever shown him when I indulged in his body without being married to him. Moreover, by getting out of an affair that was going nowhere, I cleaned my slate—making myself fully available for the man who will be my one and only.

∽∾∾

Lying in bed after a hard day of resisting temptation, you may be tempted to slip into fantasy. During that quiet time before falling asleep, I often used to masturbate.

I don't do that anymore. Not because it's sinful—though that's a good enough reason—but because I've come to realize that it's harmful to me.

In this age of AIDS and other rampant sexually transmitted diseases, many health organizations that receive government funding push masturbation as a form of "safe sex." Planned Parenthood is at the vanguard of this effort, telling youths on its Web site Teenwire that masturbation is a "dress rehearsal" for sex. Not only does it release sexual tension, Planned Parenthood says, but it also enables you to learn what excites you and therefore become better prepared for the sex act.

When my experiences of intercourse became fewer and farther between, and my experiences of masturbation increased, I did not find that masturbation was a "dress rehearsal." It became the main event—so much so that when I had sex, I was trying to duplicate the actions and fantasies that I had developed while masturbating. As a result, instead of teaching me how to enhance my physical experience of sex, masturbation actually narrowed down the means by which I could get turned on.

If a woman requires lots of bells and whistles in order to get excited, if she has to have a certain fantasy in mind, if her route to sexual satisfaction is like a set of meticulous Mapquest driving directions, she's not sexually liberated. She's sexually *imprisoned*. For all her supposed wildness and kinks, her ability to fully experience sexual pleasure is stymied by the emotional and physical restrictions she's placed upon herself.

Masturbation trains one to limit sexual expression, because it's all about the orgasm. When it becomes the model that intercourse has to emulate, the result is an orgasm-centered view of sex, where one's body and the body of one's partner become mere accessories to genital sensations.

Imagine if it were possible to take a train ride through Yellowstone National Park, one of the most beautiful places in the world. Now, imagine if that train were a 200-mph high-speed train. Through the windows, the giant redwoods and gorgeous wetlands would be all but invisible—just a dull green and brown blur. That's what intercourse is like when the overriding intention is to pay obeisance to the almighty orgasm. Sex, which should unite a husband and a wife in the most intense love attainable, is reduced to a frenzied race for the goal of mere satisfaction.

So, through masturbation, I was teaching myself to be a selfish and superficial sex partner—and for what? A few seconds of orgasm—after which I'd feel lonelier than I did before.

A little reading on biology revealed that the post-masturbation loneliness wasn't all in my head. When a man or woman reaches orgasm, a hormone called oxytocin is released into their bloodstream. In women, oxytocin is known as the "cuddle hormone," because women's oxytocin levels go up when they're simply cuddling. For that reason, and also because it's released by nursing mothers, oxytocin is believed to facilitate emotional bonding. If the hormone is released during masturbation and there's no one with whom to bond, then of course one is going to feel bereft.

∾≺≻∽

When I resist masturbation, I find—as with resisting other forms of temptation—that I gain a feeling of strength, of confidence, and even wonder.

There's a great sense of freedom when you're able to experience the world around you and have friendships with people without the constant awareness that you're being perceived as a sexual person and that you have to perceive others as sexual. You still are a red-blooded woman, of course, and you're sure to meet men you'll find attractive. However, the farther you get out of temptation mode, the more you'll be able to see men as they are—and appreciate them even more than you did before.

I now find that, more than ever, I really *like* men—and because I do, I am more confident than ever that I'll be able to sustain a loving relationship with one and marry him. The innocence that I had in the days when I could be wowed by a "Hi, toothless" is back. The only difference is, I'm a bit longer in the tooth.

seventeen

heavy mettle: mending the chinks in your spiritual armor

If your parents were hippies, there's a good chance that nestled deep in their LP collection—perhaps between well-worn copies of Crosby, Stills, Nash & Young's *Déjà Vu* and the Moody Blues' *Days of Future Passed*—lies an album whose cover features a long-haired, mustachioed man in a dress.

The man is Frank Zappa, and the album is *We're Only in It for the Money*, a 1968 effort by his group Mothers of Invention lampooning the "If it feels good, do it" philosophy of the time. One track asks, "What's the ugliest part of your body?"

The song answers its own question: "your mind."

Chastity is, first and foremost, a mental discipline. You can try to push yourself by displaying self-control when your heart isn't in it, but keeping it up over the long haul requires dedication.

Because the foundation of your chastity is within you, the greatest challenges to it lurk within as well. Some of these challenges you know all too well. They're the temptations that you have to put out of your mind—like when a handsome male acquaintance with a well-deserved reputation for womanizing suggests he'd like to get to know you better. They're also the feelings of loneliness and uncertainty— like when you spend the night home alone after politely declining the womanizer's invitation. But that's not what I have in mind just now.

It's when you feel most confident in your ability to resist temptation, and when you feel least susceptible to loneliness, that you have to be on your guard for what is spiritually the most dangerous challenge to chastity: the unexpected, utterly embarrassing, seemingly irrational obsession.

By nature, an obsession comes about when you least expect it. You may be putting your resources into projecting confidence and self-control, repressing your little-girl side that fears rejection. But that little girl still dwells in you—and she's still fascinated by men who seem unattainable.

Normally, it's possible to work your way through an obsession without much trouble. It takes prayer, determination, and keeping your eyes on the prize. On rare occasions, however, the obsession may succeed in burying its hooks deeply into your psyche—something I once learned the hard way.

A year and a half ago, I was living chastely but not particularly hopefully. I felt bored and complacent. None of the men I knew were romantic possibilities. I'd recently turned down some opportunities for casual sex, and I was feeling confident of my ability to hold out for marriage—more confident than I'd ever been before. Too confident.

There was a man at my work I'll call Ian, whom I'd known casually for a couple of years, as we traveled in the same circles. I'd always thought he was handsome and debonair, as well as being intelligent and well spoken, but he never seemed to notice me. He would walk by my desk every day and never say hello, even though we'd spoken a few times.

One day, a coworker I barely knew was leaving for another job, and my office took the opportunity to hold a send-off for him at a nearby bar. It seemed like ages since I'd been to a party, so I brought a sexy minidress to work that day and changed into it before going to the send-off. (I had yet to work out the wardrobe aspect of chastity.) Ian was there, scotch and soda in hand, and to my surprise, he struck up a conversation with me—complimenting me on my dress.

I am never so vulnerable as when a man I thought was out of my league suddenly pays me a compliment. I stayed by Ian's side for over an hour—and he didn't seem to mind.

Ian, it transpired, *really* liked his liquor. Unconsciously, I found myself returning to the old behavior I'd displayed hanging around rock musicians after concerts—I figured that if I stuck around long enough, they'd get drunk enough to want to take me home.

Needless to say, by slipping back into the familiar role of enabler, I was completely going against my better judgment. I knew on a deeper level that I wouldn't want a man who drank to get drunk, let alone one who wouldn't want me unless he'd had a few. But I was drunk—not with alcohol, but with excitement that *Ian noticed me*.

He wound up walking me the fifteen blocks downtown to where I would catch my train home. On the way, he confessed that he was lonely and suffered from depression.

Oh, I thought, *he's so vulnerable. How sweet. He must really like me, to be opening up like this.*

I told him that I used to suffer from depression myself, until I came to faith. Did he have faith? He didn't, but wished he had. In my mind, I was already imagining myself as being the girlfriend who would help him see the light.

If I allowed my better judgment to take hold, I would have known that I was fooling myself. I can't stop a man from drinking too much coffee, let alone make one stop drinking alcohol, stop being depressed, and get down on his knees to say the Sinner's Prayer. Granted, once one is in a committed relationship with a man, one must bear with his infirmities. However, I don't believe that God, in choosing the man with whom I'll make a home, intends to start me off with a "handyman's special."

Before I knew it, Ian and I were at the train station. He gave me a confused look—as though he wasn't sure whether or how he should kiss me good-bye. Then he leaned down—he was tall—to give me a lightning-fast kiss on the lips, and he was off.

I thought about Ian all the way home. Lying in bed that night, I fantasized about him. In the morning, I awoke with a mixture of hope and fear—and still, I couldn't stop thinking about him.

The hope was short-lived. Very quickly, it became clear that what I had taken as interest from Ian was really just curiosity—and that curiosity had been satisfied. He might like to occasionally have a drink with me and share his troubles, but that would be it.

Normally, upon realizing that my love interest had lost interest, I would pick myself up and move on. For reasons I didn't understand, that didn't happen. Instead, I started regressing back to the kind of mind-set I had in high school, when I feared that losing a potential boyfriend meant losing my last chance for love.

One night, since a mutual friend had invited Ian and me to a party, we met up and went there together. Upon our arrival, Ian proceeded to work the room as though I weren't there. By that point, however, I was too far gone to realize I wasn't really on a date. I didn't want to be confused by the facts.

Coming at a point when my life was so same old, same old, and congratulating myself on being so godly and chaste, I was blindsided by this obsessive attraction. Worst of all, I had to deal with it in the workplace.

I used to tolerate Ian's walking by without saying hello. Now, whenever he seemed to ignore me, I was crushed. I started wearing progressively sexier outfits to the workplace in hope of his noticing me. Then I'd pop into his office on some slim pretext, looking for a bit of conversation, but I was so nervous that I'd only wind up embarrassing myself.

After a couple of weeks of being unable to get Ian out of my mind, it started to dawn on me that I had a problem. Although I was extremely reluctant to give up my hope that he might someday fall in love with me, it was clear that I couldn't continue to have him at the center of my thoughts. I was having trouble sleeping and was often on the verge of tears. Really, I feared I was going crazy.

The worst part was that I knew on some level that my obsession wasn't rational—yet it seemed there was nothing I could do about it. I felt helpless and didn't understand why.

So I did what any self-respecting girl would have done in such a situation. I called my mom.

She listened as I told her about how I had fallen into a crush that felt terribly wrong. Even if Ian *were* right for me and liked me back, I explained, I wasn't feeling the way I was supposed to feel. Love, I knew, could make one a bit silly or uncomfortable—but not physically ill and borderline insane.

Taking my complaint very seriously, Mom advised me to read up on what Christians call spiritual warfare—especially Paul's words in 2 Corinthians, where he distinguishes between physical enemies and spiritual enemies: "For though we walk in the flesh, we do not war according to the flesh. For the weapons of our warfare are not carnal but mighty in God for pulling down strongholds, casting down arguments and every high thing that exalts itself against the knowledge of God, bringing every thought into captivity to the obedience of Christ" (10:3–5 NKJV).

Bringing every thought into captivity means being the master of one's thoughts and passions instead of being mastered by them. It made sense to me; that was what I needed to do. If Paul knew what he was talking about, then I needed help—because I was locked, however unwillingly, in a spiritual battle.

The solution, Paul advised, is to "take up the whole armor of God" (v. 13 NKJV)—which, like the weapons of the enemy, are spiritual, not physical.

Far from being imaginary protection, this spiritual armor is a set of real inner qualities that are recognized for their power to shield one from spiritual harm: truth, righteousness, preparedness, faith, salvation, and prayer.

With my emotional pain over Ian's making me feel under siege, I began a two-pronged counterattack. I prayed each day for God to cover me with spiritual armor. At the same time, I opened up to a few of my closest friends and family members, asking them to pray that I be released from my obsession.

Immediately upon beginning the counterattack, my symptoms began to ease. The choked-up feeling dissipated, as did much of my nervousness around Ian.

I asked more friends to pray for me—and told them why. I was embarrassed to admit what I was going through, but they understood. These were close friends, mind you—not ones who would gossip.

The more that people were praying for me, the more peace I began to feel, and the better able I was to don my spiritual armor. Within a week, I was back to normal. It was much longer before I could be comfortable near Ian—to this day, the memory of my obsession makes me tense up a bit around him—but at least I felt I could control myself.

As the old saying goes, the price of liberty is eternal vigilance. Chastity is true liberty—freedom from slavery to passions that are damaging or counterproductive. It's also freedom to experience passions—by choice, and not by compulsion. What I learned from my experience with obsession is that I can't take that freedom for granted. The moment one allows chinks in one's spiritual armor, the spirit of darkness will seep in like a lethal gas.

A fascinating aspect of spiritual warfare is what it demonstrates about the power of prayer. People tend to think of emotional states as being responsive only to therapy, or to a change in external circumstances. With prayer, however, we rise above the power of our physical bodies and gain access to power granted by God. If that for which we pray is God's will—and it is always God's will that evil should be defeated—then we can be confident that He will arm us with every spiritual weapon necessary for victory.

∽∾

Prayer, like any good weapon, may be used not only for defensive purposes, but for offensive as well. You can use it to take aim at your singlehood. If you believe you're ready to meet the right man and get married, that desire should be part of your prayer life.

Some people recommend simply praying night and day to be sent a husband. I wouldn't. I did that for a long time and found that not only did I not get a husband, but I was more easily deceived. When I met a possible love interest, I would think, *God is answering my prayers!* The thought would make me rush into relationships while overlooking obvious problems in compatibility.

Today, I pray for God to make me ready for marriage; to send me my husband when I'm ready; and to grant me patience in the meantime. I also thank Him for doing everything in His good time. It's hard to say such a prayer when I'm annoyed that He's taking His own sweet time, but it reminds me that experience has shown that God has a better sense of timing than I do.

Last, I ask God to bless, guide, strengthen, and protect my future husband. Praying for my future husband reminds me that God knows who he is even when I don't. It also makes me feel spiritually connected to him—even if we have yet to meet.

Praying for our heart's desire according to God's will is how we align ourselves with our purpose in life. When we make our plans without consulting God, we're like trains with faulty wheels that keep threatening to spin off the track. Something as simple as a heartfelt prayer can send us back in the direction we're supposed to be going.

Just about every day, I ride an underground train called the PATH (Port Authority Trans Hudson) into midtown Manhattan, taking a seat all the way up front by the driver's compartment, where I can see the signals. When I'm not burying my nose in a book for the thirteen-minute ride, I think about what those signals mean.

As long as the driver's on the right track, he knows where his destination is, but he can't see it while he's in the long, dark tunnel. All he can see are these little lights that blink red, green, or yellow. To me, that's like the life of one who's following God. Even when I know my goal is holiness, I still have to watch that I don't rush into things when God wants me to go slow, or stay in one place when God wants me to press on.

Once, when I had a moment to chat with the driver before the train started, I asked him, "How many signals are there between here and New York?"

"Oh, I don't know—forty, fifty," he replied.

"And you have to watch for every one," I marveled. "I really admire how you can do that—all the concentration it takes, because any one of those signals could turn into a red light."

I wasn't being sarcastic, and I don't think he took it that way. Still, he told me, in the nicest way possible, that my romanticism was ludicrous.

"It's a *boring* job," he said.

My face fell.

"It's the same thing every day. It's boring," he repeated. "I'm stuck here in this vertical coffin, on this metal seat . . ."

He went on. I tried to look sympathetic. In another moment, I was saved by the bell of the closing train doors.

I realized that when he leaves his "vertical coffin," he may think he's done watching signals for the day. His job is hard, but his life is relatively easy.

With me, it's the opposite. I love watching the train signals because they're so clear. It's when I leave the train that I worry, because God's signals become obscured by the distractions of everyday life.

So I still envy the driver for the certainty he has by way of those flashing lights. And I'm thankful for every day that God's Word gives me light on my path.

eighteen
why shared values matter

My mother likes to talk about something I said one time when I was about ten or so and she asked me what the most important quality I would look for in a boyfriend was. (At the time, it was most definitely a hypothetical question, though I admit that when I was six years old, I was briefly "married" to my classmate Greg Clayton.)

I answered, "That he likes me."

Ah, if it were only that simple, right?

My response reflected something deep inside me that remained throughout my dating life, up until very recently. I overestimated the value of a man's desire to commit to me—and underestimated my own desirability. It was a kind of superstition that affected the way I entered relationships, making me vulnerable to men who wanted an instant commitment.

First of all, any man I found appealing had the surprise factor going for him if he wanted to be in a relationship with me. It always blew my mind when someone I liked returned my interest.

Whenever I entered a relationship too quickly, there would

inevitably come a time when I would realize that my boyfriend and I disagreed about things that were important to me. Unfortunately—and this is where my superstition came up—I would often try to gloss over the differences, reasoning that the mere fact that "he liked me" should be sufficient to cover everything.

What I didn't understand then, and am beginning to understand now, is this: the only way that a man and a woman in a relationship can work out their biggest and most troublesome differences over time is if they are in love. A man and a woman can be in love only if they each love what is in the other. If a man does not love what is in me—including the values that help make me who I am—then, while he may feel a kind of love toward me, he doesn't really love me.

Real love is the *agape* love I described earlier—the kind where you're defined by what you love, rather than by what loves you. Because I believe that God is love, I believe that in a truly loving relationship, both the man and the woman love God—and so they become God's love to each other.

As the apostle Paul put it, through looking to God, we become like Him: "We, who . . . all reflect the Lord's glory, are being transformed into his likeness with ever-increasing glory, which comes from the Lord" (2 Corinthians 3:18 NIV). It's a kind of spiritual osmosis, an almost chemical reaction from being near the source of love; and like a chemical reaction, it affects every part of our being. Through it, we are renewed and we learn how to love more deeply.

So, what's the difference between the love of a man who loves you without knowing or loving God and that of one who knows the true source of his love? It's like the difference between a canal and a river.

I recently took a walk along the Delaware and Raritan Canal, in southern New Jersey near the Pennsylvania border. It's a lovely body of water, still and calm, surrounded by nature. One could be happy there for a while—if one didn't know what lay beyond.

But I wasn't satisfied just seeing the canal, because I knew there was something more just around the bend. I followed it until it finally opened up into its source—the Delaware River. *Wham!* Suddenly I had gone from a place of stillness and quietude to a grand, rushing river. Here, too, was nature—but in far greater diversity, with more kinds of flowers, trees, birds, animals, and insects. At some points, the river was bordered by rocks; at others, hanging willows.

The river's rushing ripples were far more exciting than the canal's placid stillness. Yet, if I wanted, by watching their repetitive motion for a time, I could fall into their rhythms and enjoy a feeling of relaxation.

The love that is joined only to its object is the canal. The love that is joined first to a greater source and then—through that source, to its object—is the river.

∽◦∾

Tom was frantic. After five months of dating him, I had just told him I wanted to break up. I'd been thinking about it, I explained, and realized I had made a big mistake rushing into things. As our relationship approached the critical six-month mark, it was clear to me that our differences were insurmountable: I was a Christian, and he was an atheist.

Feeling helpless, Tom (not his real name) did something outrageous. He sent an e-mail to everyone in his address book, telling them about the breakup and asking them for advice on how to convince me to stay with him. As he worked in a job that overlapped journalism, politics, and public relations, his address book included about three hundred people.

Understandably, I was *livid*. My most personal issues were laid out for journalists, magazine editors, political operatives, publicists, and hundreds of strangers with big mouths. It was painful enough for me to consider breaking up with Tom; I'd thought long and hard about it before making the decision. To suddenly find myself on a virtual stage—with people on the sidelines invited to put in their two cents—was like starring in a nightmarish reality show.

Tom forwarded me some of the responses to his plea. Among them was one from a nationally known female political columnist/TV commentator and author who had recently caused a stir with her strong views in favor of tightening immigration laws. Despite her reputation for severity, her e-mail to me was all sweetness and light. She told me that she was a religious Christian married to an atheist, and if she could do it, I could too.

I remember staring at my work computer in disbelief as I read the columnist's missive. She meant well, no doubt about that, but it just seemed so bizarre to get unsolicited advice from her on my love life.

"What's up?"

I turned and saw my coworker Jon. He'd seen me looking at my computer screen with my mouth open. He knew about Tom's letter—he'd gotten it too.

"It's an e-mail from [Ms. X]," I explained. "She responded to the one Tom sent asking people to persuade me to stay with him." I sighed. "She says I should be more open-minded."

There was a pause, and then Jon—who had read his share of Ms. X's op-eds—said incredulously, *"[Ms. X]* is telling *you* to be open-minded?"

I met Tom in the summer of 2002, when I was between two worlds. It was after I'd become a Christian, but before I'd begun living out my faith. That was the time of my "sexual safety net," when I thought that premarital sex wouldn't cause me any spiritual damage as long as I asked God for forgiveness.

The relationship began at a barbecue at a friend's house, where Tom and I hit it off right away. At thirty-two, he was a year younger than me, blond-haired and blue-eyed, looking trim and very Ivy League in his neatly pressed button-down shirt and khaki shorts. While I didn't normally go for preppy types, I liked how he seemed so gentlemanly and civilized—not like the musicians and writers I was used to being with. He also had a great sense of humor, and he knew so much about such a wide range of subjects—from Greek philosophy to American history, to British sci-fi movies—that I felt I wouldn't be bored around him.

We wound up going to a movie together that very night. I knew I was in for a good time from the chivalrous way Tom offered to carry my popcorn. Afterward, we repaired to a cozy café and talked about our belief systems. Tom was very into discussing such things, being a philosophy major.

I told him about the faith experience I'd had a few years earlier that had changed me from an agnostic Jew to a Bible-believing Christian. He told me he was a devout atheist—and he wanted to kiss me.

Against my better judgment, I kissed him. It felt pleasant—but no fireworks. That should have tipped me off right away; if a man's kiss isn't exciting, either he's not the right one, or it's too soon to be kissing him.

I didn't let the lack of fireworks stop me, because I didn't trust myself. Every other time I'd experienced fireworks, I'd been hurt. If I was able to enjoy Tom's company *without* swooning, maybe that meant it was finally the real thing. (Note to self: Next boyfriend must be swoonworthy.) Also, and I hate to admit this, being able to admire Tom's looks without being swept away gave me a feeling of control—a built-in layer of emotional protection.

What I did feel was enough to hook me. It was the possibility that this good-looking, smart, fun man might want me as a girlfriend.

Although I wasn't yet set on chastity, I knew I'd had enough of passionate friends and one-night stands. After one kiss, I confessed to Tom that I didn't kiss just to fool around anymore; a relationship was what I was after.

He said he wasn't interested in just fooling around either; it wasn't in his nature. He said it quite seriously, and although part of me felt like the most gullible woman on earth, I believed him.

It turned out that he was indeed telling the truth. In fact, as I got to know him, I learned that he was incapable of telling a lie. In the words of Bob Dylan, "To live outside the law, you must be honest." I was to learn that for a devout atheist like Tom, intent on proving he can live within society but outside God's law, ethics are essential to survival.

※ ⁓∽∾⁓ ※

From the start, Tom had many qualities that I'd dreamed of finding in a boyfriend. He was devoted and faithful, and he enjoyed introducing me to his many friends. It had been so long since I'd been treated like a girlfriend and not just a pal or lover, and I relished the feeling.

At first, we got around our religious differences by playing the "live and let live" game. I could keep my prayers to myself, and Tom could try not to say anything about how all religious faith was based on superstition. That last part was very hard for him, as he was a lifetime subscriber to the *Skeptical Inquirer* and idolized professional antireligionists like James Randi.

Not surprisingly, we weren't able to live and let live for long. Even before our truce inevitably evaporated into bickering over the Bible, something didn't feel right.

I began to notice that although Tom was unusually kind and loyal to his friends, he didn't seem to particularly care about anyone else. He was polite to all, but very much in his own world. The closest he got to expressing concern over strangers was his interest in politics, but even there he tended to be more concerned about dangers to large economic entities than dangers to individuals.

I felt that something was missing from my relationship with Tom, but I didn't know what it was.

One day, in an effort to fill the gap, I asked Tom if he would consider volunteering with me. A friend of mine volunteered for a charity that delivered hot meals to elderly shut-ins on Saturday mornings; maybe she, Tom, and I could do it together.

Tom responded with a lengthy lecture. The gist of it was that the capitalist system works by enabling citizens to choose how to use their time; he did not choose to use his time volunteering; therefore, other citizens were free to volunteer in his place. He also stated that while he was personally opposed to donating his time, he gave society other intangible benefits by writing articles that supported the capitalist system.

In other words, he gave at the office.

My mind got a bit muddled trying to reconcile this seemingly heartless Scrooge with the sweet, gentle, handsome man who was always there for his friends. Hoping to find some corner of his heart that was open to faith, I started to share with him about how God had healed my depression.

Tom listened to me give my testimony as one would humor a child telling about the tooth fairy. He was willing to believe that I'd been depressed, and that I was now better—but he insisted God had nothing to do with it. Whatever change had taken place was purely psychological—the result of my own gullibility and positive thinking, he said.

The more Tom denied that God was responsible for what I believed were the fruits of my faith, the more distant I felt from him. I tried to explain to him what was wrong, but it seemed there was no way I could make him understand. To him, I was just being unreasonable. He insisted he loved me, and he made every effort he could to satisfy me—short of changing his beliefs.

Tom and I didn't break up so much as part in opposite directions. It was clear that neither of us was going to change the other. I resolved never again to date an atheist—especially one who wasn't above using his e-mail list as a bully pulpit. He resolved to never again date a theist.

～∞～

To understand what really went on between Tom and me, and what it says about the importance of shared values, I offer an allegory. Like all my favorite allegories, it involves fattening food:

Just Desserts

One beautiful morning, I woke up and found a tray full of unbaked cookies on my windowsill, all perfectly formed and ready to be baked.

As I looked at the tray in amazement, I heard a beautiful voice in my head—the voice of a perfect Being. It said, "I love you, I care about you, and I will give you a tray of cookies every morning for the rest of your life. All you have to do is bake them."

I wondered if I was going crazy, but I baked the cookies anyway and tried them. They were delicious—so much better than anything I could have created myself. I had to share them with everyone I knew—and I did.

My life started to change. I never before felt as though I had so much to give. I could share all the cookies I had, and they would always be replenished in the morning. For once, I felt I had a purpose.

When I met Tom, the first thing I did was offer him one of my cookies. He was enthralled and had to have more.

I gave Tom more cookies—and told him about how they appeared on my windowsill every morning, given to me by Someone I couldn't see, who loved me very much. My only contribution was putting them in the oven and taking them out in time.

"That's impossible," Tom said. He had sometimes noticed my taking a tray of batter from my windowsill, but assumed it was some odd baker's trick of leaving the dough out overnight. In any case, he wasn't interested enough in my cookies' origin to do the research necessary to discover where they came from.

"How can it be impossible?" I asked. "Where else would the cookies come from? I never used to get them before."

He had heard about such things, he said. In every case, the origin of the mysterious cookies turned out to be a figment of the baker's imagination.

"What are you talking about?" I exclaimed. "You tasted them. They're real."

"Yes," he said, "the cookies themselves are real—but they didn't come from some imaginary being. You made them."

"But I told you I found them!" I protested. "Are you calling me a liar?"

"No," he said.

"Then you're calling me crazy?"

"No, not at all. You're making the cookies unconsciously. There is a known psychological condition by which an otherwise sane person has a mental block, so that she forgets the time she spends each day making cookies."

"Now, that's crazy," I said. "Think about it: What's more probable— that I'm getting the cookie dough from Someone else, or that my otherwise sane mind is completely erasing the fact that I'm making it myself?"

We argued for a while longer, with Tom using my personal weaknesses to score points. He observed that some mornings I didn't bake cookies at all, and some mornings I burned the cookies and they were no good. In both instances, it was through my own fault or neglect—there was nothing wrong with the dough I had been given. However, he took my not baking them perfectly every day as evidence that they came from me—and not from a perfect Being. After all, he reasoned, if a perfect Being made them, they would always be perfect.

Exasperated, I left off arguing for a while. Tom tried to make me feel better. He baked me some cookies of his own—good ones too. He was quite proud of all the effort he put into them and kept most of them for himself, though he was generous to me and others in his inner circle.

As Tom and I tried to patch things up, I suggested an experiment. It would mean a lot to me, I said, if we would share the experience of baking cookies together.

And so, one morning, the two of us gathered in the kitchen—me with my ready-made dough from the windowsill, and him with his own batter recipe. We tried to combine the two, expecting an amazing new flavor sensation—one of those magical chocolate-meets-peanut-butter moments.

It was not to be.

My dough and his refused to mix. They had different densities, and no matter how much we needed—I mean, kneaded—them together, they always separated.

There's more to the story, but I'll leave off here for now.

The dough is God's grace, or rather, graces. He gives each of us unique graces every day: "His compassions . . . are new every morning" (Lamentations 3:22–23 NKJV). The act of baking represents my works—what I do with the graces I have been given. I can choose whether and how to develop and share those graces.

Tom's baking cookies from his own dough is performing works without faith—for if he had faith, he would have the grace that comes by faith, and would not need to attempt to create his own.

The works Tom creates are sufficient for getting by in this world, but they do not mix with faith, because he refuses to cede to God's lordship. He would rather create all his works by himself from scratch—even if they prove inferior and incompatible with those produced by faith—than allow God to work through him.

The rest of the story has yet to be written—but I know how it ends.

One day, I am going to meet a man who appeals to me on every level—including that of values. He'll know what it's like to receive graces every morning, and he'll want to share his, just as I want to share mine. More than that, as we continue in faith, his graces will combine with mine so that we will become greater than the sum of our parts. The two of us will cleave to each other and become one flesh.

Or, at the very least, we'll have delicious homemade cookies to send to our friends come Christmastime . . .

nineteen
seeing is believing:
holding on to your vision

For a few months when I was between jobs, I did medical billing for my stepfather, an eye doctor who specializes in low-vision patients. I learned something there: people who are losing their eyesight are not a particularly happy bunch.

My stepfather is, by contrast, one of the most relentlessly upbeat people I have ever met. A Jew who converted to Christianity during his mid-forties, he bubbles with evangelical fervor, always ready to share the good news with his patients. To him, faith is essential to healing.

Some of his patients listen. Others want only prescriptions, not Scriptures. For them, my stepfather refrains from mentioning God—but his warm disposition betrays his inner light. He refuses to give up on cases that other doctors deem hopeless—and he exhorts his patients not to give up on themselves.

Working in my stepfather's office and watching how his patients responded to his encouragement, I saw that those who got the most out of treatment were the ones who were the most hopeful, no matter how bleak their prognosis.

It's the old "power of positive thinking" principle. The patients who came in with a dark cloud over their heads were unlikely to improve much no matter what my stepfather tried to do for them. The ones who got better were the ones who had faith—if not in God, then at least in the treatment. They didn't have to have a lot of faith to see results either. Just a little could make a world of difference—even a grain of faith the size of a mustard seed.

It became clear to me that the greatest danger my stepfather's patients faced was not physical blindness, but spiritual blindness. As the physical darkness closed in, the spiritual darkness loomed as well—a "darkness which may even be felt" (Exodus 10:21 NKJV).

My stepfather's patients were waging their war against blindness on two fronts. One of them—the physical front—was not always winnable. The other, vastly more important front could be won—but the soldiers were often demoralized, unaware of the powerful arms at their disposal.

Although my own eyesight is fine (with contact lenses), I know what it's like to lose one's spiritual vision. I also know what it's like to get it back. The feelings are as different as night and day.

～∞～

I am typing this from a retreat house near the Delaware River, where I have come to write. The house is run by a pair of nuns who have retired from teaching. One of them, Sister Gerry, has been blind since the age of twenty-four due to a genetic disorder. Now eighty-two, she is remarkably vibrant, despite having cancer.

Have you ever met someone who positively *radiated* grace? I've had that experience on rare occasions, nearly always in the presence of someone old and frail. It seems that God gives something extra to older people who are suffering pain or a disability—if they're open to receiving it.

Sister Gerry has that inner glow of one who has asked the Lord with all her heart to make her an instrument of His love and peace. Her eyes sparkle in a way that I've never witnessed in a blind person.

The other day, I discussed with Sister Gerry a book she had cowritten about the founder of her religious order, Lucy Filippini, called *Forever Yes: The Story of Lucy Filippini*. A copy of the book was in my room at the retreat, and I'd begun reading about how the shy young woman living in seventeenth-century Italy reacted when the church asked her to direct schools for girls and women.

Lucy went through an intense, dark period of soul-searching, feeling uncertain of God's will. Finally, feeling no comfort or consolation despite her prayers, she stepped out in faith—"quivering" out a "yes," as the book puts it.

Once Lucy made the decision to accept the daunting task, her comfort and consolation returned. But she had to take that first step on her own.

The story reminded me so much of my own life—times when, feeling trapped in darkness, I had taken a halting step out into the light. I might have felt stuck in an unsatisfying job or relationship, or just in a rut.

My experience of darkness could include fear of disappointment, fear of failing publicly, fear of ridicule—or all of the above. Most of all, I feared that there might be *nothing* out there for me—no job, or boyfriend, or life worth living, outside the familiar unhappiness that had become unbearable. When you're facing that kind of hopelessness, you need more than ordinary strength to open the door that leads to a life of hope and opportunity.

Pastor David Ireland has a good analogy [[SOURCE?]]to describe what it's like to put one's faith in action. He says it's like being a child on the third floor of a burning building, looking down and seeing a strong man with open arms. The man is saying, "Jump!"

You look at the man and you know that he is capable of catching you. You look back and you see the fire getting closer. Yet, simply knowing that the man is capable of catching you doesn't make it easy to jump.

The fire keeps getting closer, and the man keeps calling, "Jump! I'll catch you!"

Finally, when you're certain that staying in the building one moment longer will kill you, you let go of your uncertainty and ter-ror—and jump.

During the times in my life when I had to jump, God was always there to catch me. But, like the child in Pastor Ireland's story—and like Lucy Filippini—I endured a terrifying moment as I leaped into the air, before I could land safely in His everlasting arms.

I told Sister Gerry of the memories that her description of Lucy's anguish—and the eventual comfort she received—brought back to me. Then she told me that she had drawn upon personal experience as she and her coauthor, a fellow nun, wrote that part of the book.

It was her reaction to becoming blind.

"I realized I had a choice," she said.

Either she could believe her life was over, she explained—or she could say yes to blindness, and trust in what God had in store for her.

Looking at Sister Gerry—seeing her deep brown eyes with their improbable sparkle—I couldn't doubt that she had made the right choice. She had given so much to the world—and still had so much to give. Her existence alone was a gift.

In January 2006, reporter Alan Olifson of the *Ventura County Reporter* looked back on professional psychics' predictions for 2005. He found a couple of correct predictions—one psychic foresaw an increased drowning of polar bears due to higher Arctic temperatures—but was overall "not impressed."

One psychic, Kent Boxberger, had written that 2005 would contain a series of calamities—a "shocking" change of U.S. presidents, a worse terrorist attack than 9/11, the most devastating stockmarket crash ever, and hospitals going bankrupt—followed by the Braves beating the Padres to go to the World Series. Olifson drily noted, "That we could even manage to have a World Series in Boxberger's apocalyptic future is, I guess, the one thing that kept him going."

The psychics' confidence in their predictive abilities makes them easy targets of ridicule. Likewise, it's the times when we are most certain we can see what lies ahead of us that our blindness is most apparent. Think of the farsighted cartoon character Mr. Magoo, so certain that he knows what he's doing—until he tries to brush his teeth with the cat's tail.

There's a psalm that says to God, "Your word is a lamp to my feet" (Psalm 119:105 NKJV). If you've walked on garden paths lit by lamps placed on the ground, you know that such lamps only show you the next step. That's the way it is with God, and it's why I have to follow the apostle Paul's saying: "We walk by faith, not by sight" (2 Corinthians 5:7 NKJV). The only way to stay out of darkness is to realize my total dependence on the Lord and trust that His Word will always give me enough light to keep me from falling into a ditch.

But sight is much more than just being able to see what's in front of you. By itself, that's only tunnel vision. To gain a full perspective on your environment, you also need to be able to perceive peripherally.

Spiritually speaking, our peripheral vision is the light we receive when we reach out to others. It's the light of God's love—the love that He enables us to give and then receive back, reflected in the other person. Like all indirect light, it may not be bright enough to provide full illumination. But even so, it remains powerful enough to reveal the hidden beauty in every corner of our lives.

There's a fable that's a staple of sermons, about the man who receives from God a glimpse of hell and a glimpse of heaven. Hell is a room full of desperately starving people, and in the midst of them is a bowl of delicious-smelling stew. All the people have spoons, but their spoons have such long handles that it's impossible for them to feed themselves.

Heaven is a room with an identical-looking bowl of stew at its center. Everyone there also has long spoons, but all the people are happy and content.

When the man glimpsing heaven asks God how the people there can be so happy while the ones under identical circumstances in hell are suffering, God replies, "They feed one another."

It's a simple truth, but one that's easy to forget when you're lonely and feeling sorry for yourself. When you can't see what's in front of you, you need to get some reflected light into your life. The way to get that light is through reaching out to others.

It doesn't require extraordinary effort. You don't have to go out and save the world.

What it does require is a conscious decision—a decision to align your will with God's will for you.

This is not the same as merely resigning yourself to God's will.

In fact, it's the opposite. Being resigned means simply signing off on something in which one has no hope of having an active role.

Instead of passive resignation, one must commit to *active resolution*: the determination to never miss an opportunity to experience God's grace, or miss an opportunity to share His grace with others.

This is something that can be done every minute of every day. God's grace may be found in every experience, whether it's a happy or painful one. We discover His grace by stepping out in faith—realizing our dependence on the Lord, and allowing ourselves to risk disappointment, so that we might be open to every blessing He has in store for us.

Our culture misunderstands the nature of disappointment. Advertisers try to convince us to buy brand-name products rather than risk disappointment by taking a chance on unknown brands. Women's magazines tell us to give an attractive, available man a chance in the sack—whether or not we love him—rather than risk an untold number of lonely nights waiting for a husband who may never arrive. Always, we are warned that this may be our last chance. Like the advertising tagline that warns, "This offer will expire in 30 days," we're told that our odds of being married will expire after we hit age thirty.

What do we do when faced with this fear? We go spiritually blind and grab at the air, like the frantic game-show contestant in a glass booth who has thirty seconds to snatch as many one-hundred-dollar bills as she can. We latch on to the first nonrepulsive man who breezes our way and end up facing just what we were trying so hard to avoid—disappointment.

It is the fear of disappointment that disappoints. The happiest, most fulfilled people are those who have overcome this fear. Only then are they free to display all the graces that have been given them. They have hope, and, as Paul wrote, "hope does not disappoint" (Romans 5:5 NKJV).

The other night I had dinner with a male friend, a charming English journalist I would date if he shared my faith (he doesn't) and if he were interested in getting married (ditto). He peppered me with questions about chastity, even going so far as to suggest that maybe, given that I'd been looking for so long, I might not find the man I was looking for.

"That's not true," I responded. "My chances are better now than they've ever been, because before I was chaste, I was looking for love in all the wrong places. It's only now that I'm truly ready for marriage and have a clear vision of the kind of man I want for my husband.

"I may be thirty-seven," I concluded, "but in husband-seeking years, I'm only twenty-two."

~~~

Some people spend long hours praying for a sign to show them what they're meant to do with their lives. A particular word might come to them in prayer—a friend of mine once got the word *Philadelphia*—and then they'll spend more hours praying to discern what *that* means.

Personally, although I myself have prayed for guidance at times when I've been unsure of which direction to take, I don't believe it normally takes any great effort to discern God's will. Once we begin to realize our complete dependence on Him for all things, striving to recognize and share the grace He gives us, God gives us a sure sign that our will is aligned with His.

The sign is gratitude—our own gratitude.

The word comes from *gratus*, the Latin word for "grace." When we recognize God's grace, we are grateful. It is a spiritual reflex, as natural as a kitten's purr when you stroke it.

This gratitude comes regardless of our condition in life. No matter what we are experiencing, good or bad, as long as we can find a reason to thank God in the midst of it, we are in communication with the divine.

If you're unhappy, showing gratitude to God can ultimately help you find a way out of your troubles, as I discovered during a long period of unemployment. It was 2002, during the depths of the recession. I prayed every day for a job, but when none of my efforts to find one panned out, it was hard to keep my hopes up.

One day, saying my morning prayers as I walked to the train station so I could "pound the pavement" in New York City, a different prayer than usual came to mind: "Thank You, God, for all the things You've done in my life, thank You for all the things You're doing in my life, and thank You for all the things You *will do* in my life."

There was something about the feeling of thanking God in advance that changed my perspective. I didn't feel like a victim anymore. No matter what happened, I felt secure that God had everything in hand. More than that, I believed He would enable me to be an active participant in His plan.

If I had known back in 2002 that I'd have the wonderful job I have now, the long period of unemployment would have been a breeze. No time of hardship is so difficult when you know it has a happy ending. That's why I'm determined to apply the same philosophy to my single state. I've nothing to lose by assuming it has a happy ending—and everything to gain.

The time God gives you to be single is precious, and not merely because you have more freedom than a married woman to do what you want to do when you want to do it. It's precious because you have a unique opportunity to bring all your spiritual graces to full flower—and to do so in a way that will bear fruit for the rest of your life.

This season of your life when you are single isn't winter. It's *springtime*.

∽◦∾

When we bring ourselves in line with God's will for us, we open up the conduit so that He may touch us, and so give us a glimpse of eternity. As best-selling author Joni Eareckson Tada, a quadriplegic, has said, "The best we can hope for in this life is a knothole peek at the shining realities ahead. Yet a glimpse is enough. It's enough to convince our hearts that whatever sufferings and sorrows currently assail us aren't worthy of comparison to that which waits over the horizon."[13]

I believe you have already seen that glimpse, whether you realize it or not. It is the hope for something better that has made you pick up this book, and that hope was put there by God. As stated in Ecclesiastes, He has set eternity in your heart. Hold tight to that glimpse of heaven and you will find that even when you're at your lowest point, little rays of light will brighten the dark corners of your life.

It's the times when we feel most in need of God's love that life can feel, as writer Jim Friedland once said, like "that most merry, absurd and bewildering chase . . . in which what you are pursuing with fear and desperation is what seeks you with love."[14]

Always remember that you are not alone. God seeks you. As the apostle John wrote, "We love Him because He first loved us" (1 John 4:19 NKJV). Living in faith is the thrill of the *chased*. And it starts now.

from willpower to thrill power

When one friend of mine heard the title of this book, she assumed it was going to be about drawing energy and excitement from repressed sexual desires—what Sigmund Freud called "sublimation."

Far be it from me to contradict the father of modern psychiatry, but I don't believe that refraining from sex necessarily leaves one with oodles of pent-up urges just waiting to be redirected. If that were true, then by now, given my capacity for sexual excitement, I would have done something *big*. *Really* big. I mean, I would have either saved the world or, failing that, built the largest rubber-band ball known to man.

The thrill of the chaste is something else entirely.

∽∾

The Freudian concept that sexual frustration may be turned toward "higher" goals assumes there is something in the nature of sexual frustration that is essentially good.

Now, there is good to be found in sexual desire. The capacity for it is an essential part of our makeup. Likewise, there is good contained in the desire for eating and drinking. Sex, however, is different from eating and drinking in that it is not necessary for an individual's survival. Because of this, we are able to control our desire for sex to a far greater extent than we can control our desire for food and drink.

Sexual frustration—as opposed to ordinary sexual desire—means being preoccupied with the unfulfilled desire for sex, to the point where it takes precedence over other desires or otherwise interferes with one's mental health. The equivalent in terms of eating or drinking would be an addiction that causes one to obsess over a substance that would not be harmful in moderation—but, again, is not really needed to live. For example, it's natural to desire something to drink, but not to crave a particular mind-altering drink so much that it impairs one's ability to function.

When you meet a friend with an alcohol problem who's now making a sincere go at kicking the habit, you don't say to her, "Just think of all the things you can do with your alcoholic frustration now that you're able to put it to good use." The frustration that accompanies the alcoholic's craving may be a powerful force, but it's a negative one. It can't create. It can only destroy.

The power that an alcoholic receives when she quits drinking comes not from frustration but from self-control. In our consumer culture, we have been taught that self-control and frustration are essentially the same; the first leads to the second. If you exercise self-control, the TV commercials say, you will be frustrated, so why fight it? As the old potato-chip ad slogan goes, "Betcha can't eat just one." It's not in advertisers' interest to suggest that temporary self-denial can lead to greater reward.

The truth is, when you use self-control to hold out for what you really desire, you don't become frustrated. You become *empowered*.

Frustration comes from resentment, and resentment comes from pride. The frustrated ego says, "I deserve this, and I am being denied it for reasons that are beyond my control."

What is it, exactly, that we *deserve* in life?

For example, do I deserve to have a job? Sure, if an employer wants to hire me. I deserve to have my current job because I do it well. Did I deserve it before I got it? Strictly speaking, no.

We've all seen what happens when we vote a seemingly capable politician into office, who seems perfectly deserving of election, only to discover the skills that made the candidate a great campaigner don't make him or her a great elected official. In the same way, until I started to work at my current job, no one could know for certain how I might do at it, no matter how much I had accomplished at other positions. I didn't deserve the job any more than an excellent driver deserves to get a driver's license without taking the road test. The job was given to me, and I proved myself deserving.

I side with the Founding Fathers, who, expounding on truths they derived from the Bible, recognized some of humanity's basic, inalienable rights as "life, liberty, and the pursuit of happiness."

We all deserve life and liberty because of our nature as human beings created with free will. Having free will, however, doesn't mean we're always entitled to exercise it the way we'd like, which is why the Constitution's framers wrote that we have a right to the *pursuit* of happiness. They didn't write simply "happiness"—because we don't always deserve what we pursue.

The word *deserve* comes from the Latin *deservire*, which means "to serve zealously." You can serve only something that's already there—not an imagined cause or person.

I deserve to be able to seek a husband. The desire for marriage is a cause of mine, and I serve it zealously, striving every day to be ring-worthy. I do not deserve a husband.

And you know what? I wouldn't have it any other way.

We've all seen the spoiled rich young heirs and heiresses who seem unable to enjoy anything because it's all given to them. In their minds, they *deserve* to wear only the most expensive designer clothing and jewelry, to live in mansions, and to party five nights out of the week because they don't have to be at a job in the morning.

Yet, despite their material advantages and their sense of entitlement, many children of wealth remain bored and frustrated, turning to drugs or sex—which still doesn't satisfy them. Frustration cannot be converted into a higher purpose, because it derives from the false notion of entitlement. We don't appreciate that which we believe we deserve.

When I meet my husband, I will appreciate him as the gift that he is—and I know he will appreciate me in the same way. It's because we won't deserve each other that we will both seek with all our hearts to *become* deserving, fulfilling our mission as husband and wife.

Beyond the sense of entitlement, there's something else in the makeup of frustration that makes it a negative force no matter what the ends to which it's directed. Frustration is based on the concept of gratification: "I want sex, I will get it, and I will be satisfied—until I want it again." Contrast this with self-control, which says, "I want to be married, I will behave as one who is worthy of marriage, and when I am married, I will continue to work at it." Self-control looks to satisfying one's hopes, but it never wishes to be completely sated, because it knows that the object of its desire is not a thing to be consumed.

The state of mind that made me open to premarital sex was, consumerist by its nature. I viewed the world in terms of objects and people to be desired and, I hoped, acquired and used. I was not an intentionally cruel person, and I would never have consciously thought of myself as using others, but the fact remains that I treated men as things to be had.

The consumerist philosophy extended to the rest of my life. I lived in rhythms that were similar to the wham-bam rhythms of casual sex: the buildup, the excitement, the quiet period afterward, the inevitable end.

Impatience was part of my makeup; I always wanted to push on to the next big thing, whatever it might be. As I was not one to stop and smell the flowers, many opportunities to experience beauty passed me by. I'm ashamed to say that when I lived on West Eighty-eighth Street just off Central Park West for a year and a half after graduating college, not once did I walk the two blocks to the Eighty-sixth Street transverse and take a stroll through New York's greatest natural landmark.

What's worse, I even took a perverse pride in not visiting the park. Central Park, I thought, was for yuppies, sentimental old fogies, young mothers with strollers, and homeless people with nowhere else to go. I was too busy doing important things, like seeing hip bands in grimy, smoke-filled East Village rock clubs.

Today, living chastely, I live at a different pace. I don't feel such a need to *get* something out of people and things. Freed from the cycle of instant gratification, I'm more capable of experiencing them fully, in due time. As a result, my relationships with friends and family are deeper, and I receive more happiness from them—and I believe it's largely because I have so much more to give.

My ability to receive has also increased, because I'm relating to people on a deeper level. I used to assume that men were interested in me only on a superficial level. As a result, when they treated me with more dignity than they would treat a mere fling—opening a door for me, or pulling out a chair from a table so I could sit down—I didn't know how to take it. The thought was nice, but the action seemed a bit corny and unnecessary.

Now that I'm living chastely, I find myself in the highly enjoyable position of learning how to let men be gentlemen. It's a new experience, having to resist the instinct to pull my chair out on my own or open a door myself. If the man I'm with wants to do those things, I should let him—and drink in the feeling of being treated like a lady.

Chastity brings many blessings, but if it's a thrill you're after, the greatest thrill of the chaste is the gift of wonder.

My happiest moments are when I wonder at the blessings God has given me, from the smallest to the largest. I'm truly thankful for them because I don't deserve them; they're gifts.

In this day and age, wonder is a quality that's reserved for the moment one opens an exciting birthday present, or the experience of watching a big-budget film with special effects. It wasn't always like that. In an earlier time, novelists and poets recognized wonder as an essential part of what it means to be human—something that should permeate everyday life.

The nineteenth-century English poet Gerard Manley Hopkins wrote a poem titled "Pied Beauty," which exclaimed, "Glory be to God for dappled things." It's hard to imagine a modern-day poet or pop songwriter expressing such a sentiment; why thank God just because something has spots? Yet, reading Hopkins's poem, it's clear that we in the twenty-first century, who have marginalized wonder to the world of consumer products, are missing out on something unspeakably beautiful. Glory be to God, Hopkins writes, for:

All things counter, original, spare, strange,
Whatever is fickle, freckled (who knows how?)
With swift, slow; sweet, sour; adazzle, dim.

It's a shame that our age has shut wonder out of everyday life, because there are things all around us that have the potential to fill us with wonder—if only we allow ourselves to experience them and be thankful for them.

These everyday wonders can come from natural beauty like that which inspired Hopkins, or they can come from simple pleasures. Nearly every day, for example, I eat a rosemary sourdough ciabatta roll on my way to work. I pick it up from a gourmet shop and take it with me onto the commuter train, where I sneak bites of it when the conductor isn't looking and wash them down with gulps of iced tea. (Eating isn't allowed on the train, but I'm such a rebel.) My method to avoid leaving crumbs is to stick my hands into the plastic bag containing the roll and break the roll into little pieces. Then I gingerly pull the pieces out one by one. It feels good to tear at that thick crust and reach the soft inside, which contrasts with the exterior like the flesh of an exotic fruit.

As the sourdough sensation drifts across my taste buds, I savor the pieces as though they are the last such delicacy I will ever eat in my life. Indeed, they are the best thing I will have until I have another one the next day.

That's just a few short minutes out of my day. On a good day, there are many more moments like those. Many of them don't involve food. Being faced with such undeserved gifts, the idea that someone might choose a life of frustration over a life of thankfulness and appreciation is hard to fathom. In the words of G. K. Chesterton, "I wonder at not wondering."

When I was in second grade, I had a teacher who insisted that students give out valentines to everyone in the class—not just their friends—on Valentine's Day. It was an ill-considered move to keep unpopular students from feeling left out.

As one who's always been in with the out crowd, I should have benefited from the teacher's valentine system. But I didn't. The valentines I received didn't make me feel special, because I knew that whoever gave them to me was also giving them to everyone else. There was no element of surprise, no sense that my cards were gifts intended just for me.

I would rather receive one real valentine from someone giving it to me from the heart, than receive a million from people sending them out of a sense of obligation.

Before I was chaste, when I was giving off signals that I was sexually available, interest from men didn't mean to me what it means now. I was still happy when a man I found attractive found me attractive, but there was a definite sense of causation: I'm wearing a low-cut blouse, I'm saying hello to this man before he says hello to me, I'm smiling seductively and making eye contact with him, touching his shoulder, touching his arm, fluttering my eyelashes, and so on. With all those "I'm available" cues, of course he'll flirt back if he's available and finds me the least bit attractive.

Now when I receive interest from a man who interests me, it's far more exciting. I'm no longer carrying a neon sign that reads "Easy," nor am I playing hard to get. I'm dressing in a way that plays up my beauty while retaining a sense of mystery. Most of all, I'm being who I am, striving to display all the spiritual graces that have been given me. If a desirable man sees all these things and is drawn to me because of them, then there's a real chance that what attracts him most is something inside me—something that will still be there when my wrinkles multiply.

That kind of attraction is the one special valentine. You only need to receive it once in your life—and it's yours forever.

notes

1. David Thomson, "Doris Day: The cutest blonde of them all," The Independent newspaper (London), March 28, 1999.

2. Alan Vanneman, "Are Rock and Doris Hollywood's strangest romantic team?" *Bright Lights Film Journal*, issue 24, http://72.14.207.104/search?q=cache:hDTUP3wQg_8J:www.brightlightsfilm.com/24/pillowtalk1.html+%22i+knew+doris+day+before+she+was+a+virgin%22&hl=en&gl=us&ct=clnk&cd=2.

3. Mark Lowery, "Chastity Before Marriage: A Fresh Perspective," *The Catholic Faith* (May, 1998): 14-16.

4. John Zmirak and Denise Matychowiak, "Contraception, Bulimia, and Frankenfoods," Godspy.com

5. G.K. Chesterton, *The Everlasting Man*. New York: Dodd, Mead & Company, Inc., 1925.

6. Philip Yancey, *Soul Survivor: How My Faith Survived the Church*. New York: Doubleday, 2001.

7. G.K. Chesterton, *Tremendous Trifles*. London: Methuen, 1909.

8. Augustine, *Confessions*. Public Domain.

9. 1998 episode of *Sex and the City*, http://www.imdb.com/title/tt0159206/quotes.

10. Israel Abraham, *The Book of Delight and Other Papers*. New York: Arno Press, reprinted 1980.

11. C.S. Lewis, *The Great Divorce.*

12. Peter Kreeft, *Fundamentals of the Faith.* San Francisco: Ignatius Press, 1988, 181-87.

13. Joni Eareckson Tada, *HopeKeepers Magazine,* Nov.-Dec. 2004, http://www.restministries.org/hk_mag/11_12_2004/cover.htm.

14. from an e-mail

acknowledgments

It was WMCA-AM radio host Kevin McCullough whose on-air encouragement of budding bloggers first inspired me to turn my blog, The Dawn Patrol (dawneden.com/blogger.html), into a virtual soapbox for my views on values, faith, and politics. It was there, in my blog, that many of the chapters in this book got their start. My heartiest thanks go to Kevin, and to all of The Dawn Patrol's regular readers and commenters. Your support and encouragement mean more than I can say.

Very special thanks to Andrew Krucoff, who boosted my profile when he interviewed me in August 2004 for Gawker.com, and George Gurley of the *New York Observer*, who interviewed me in February 2005 after I lost my job at the *New York Post*. I'm grateful to Greg Daniel of W Publishing Group, who spotted the *Observer* piece and approached me about writing a book. And I'm grateful, too, to Michael Cooke and Martin Dunn, who also saw George's article and offered me a job at the *Daily News* that was far better than the one I had lost.

Thanks to Janet Rosen, who has been a treasured friend for ten years longer than she's been my agent, and to the friends who read my manuscript and offered revisions, especially Caren Lissner and the one who's too modest to let me thank him publicly.

Thanks to Mom, Dad, my sister, my brother, my stepmother and stepfather, all my family and friends, and my colleagues at the *Daily News*. Thanks to all those in the world of Christian media and non-profits who have enriched my life so much, especially James M. Kushiner and everyone at *Touchstone* magazine, and the American Chesterton Society.

Special thanks to Danny McKee, wherever you are, who fulfilled my seemingly impossible wish for a date to my high-school prom.

Thanks to my patron saint, Maximilian Kolbe, and to all the clergy and religious who encouraged me as I wrote this book, especially Sister Josephine Aparo and Sister Geraldine Calabrese of Morning Star House of Prayer.

Finally, very special thanks to Col Allan and Susan Edelman of the *New York Post*, without whom this book would not exist. When I think of you, I think of Genesis 50:20.